MALABAR SERIES
WYNAD

DEPUTY COLLECTOR'S OFFICE, MANANTODDY.

MALABAR SERIES
WYNAD

ITS PEOPLES AND TRADITIONS

C. GOPALAN NAIR

GYAN

Published by

Gyan Publishing House
5, Ansari Road
Daryaganj, New Delhi-110002
Phone: 011-47034999, 9811692060
E-mail: books@gyanbooks.com

Distribution Network
gyanbooks.com
India, USA, Canada, UK, Australia, France

ISBN : 978-81-212-4231-8 (PB)
First Published, Madras, 1911

2nd Impression 2020

Printed at: Gyan Press, Delhi.

Malabar Series Wynad
Author: C. Gopalan Nair

MALABAR SERIES

Wynad: ITS PEOPLES AND TRADITIONS

BY

RAO BAHADUR C. GOPALAN NAIR

Deputy Collector, Malabar

FIRST EDITION: ONE THOUSAND

Madras:

Higginbotham & Co.

1911

To

R. B. WOOD, ESQ., I. C. S.

Collector of Malabar,

CALICUT.

DEAR SIR,

I beg leave to dedicate this work to you, as a mark of esteem and respect for your sympathy with the people of Malabar, and for your unvarying kindness to me.

Yours sincerely,

CALICUT
15th November 1910.

C. GOPALAN NAIR.

To

RAO BAHADUR C. GOPALAN NAIR AVL.

MY DEAR GOPALAN NAIR,

I received your letter of dedication with much pleasure, and feel it is an honour to which the length of my service in Malabar has scarcely entitled me. The District is so large, so distinct from the rest of the Presidency, and so full of diversities within itself, that four years are all too short a period to give me a real knowledge of it. The Wynad alone is full of problems, which you have well brought out in your very interesting book. I specially admire the careful and detailed way in which you have worked out the probable origins of the different castes, by their present habits and customs. Refugees from Malabar, from Coorg, from Mysore and from the south, all found an asylum in these hills, and it is remarkable how their ways still betray them.

I venture to express my very strong hope that you will not stop, now that you have entered on the literary path. If Wynad is interesting, the plains of Malabar are infinitely more so. In Wynad you have to trace your history from legends, most of them already disappearing: in the plains you have ready to hand the "Granthams" of the old Houses, the actual daily diary of the daily life of the ancient people and Princes of Malabar. I do not know, and I have met no one who can tell me, exactly how far back these Granthams go: but I understand that it is for several hundred years, from beyond the time when Vasco de Gama first came to India, perhaps from beyond the time when the Chinese first sent their annual fleets to Quilon and Calicut. These records are of priceless historical interest: yet the cadjan files are tied up and bundled away in old cupboards and almyrahs, ready to be the prey of the first fire that chances.

I can imagine no more entrancing work than the study of these old documents. Look at Logan's marvellous chapters on the history of Malabar: and his numerous references to the traditions and legends still current. His history is little more than a bird's-eye sketch, but it is full of suggestion and possibilities. The detail of the picture still remains to be painted in, and how much of this detail is hid in these musty cadjans? The task of revealing their secrets is a great one. It requires a knowledge of the traditions of places, of the legends of families, of the old and fast disappearing customs and ceremonies. It demands industry, enthusiasm and the spirit of modern critical research. It wants an intimate and scholarly knowledge of all the *nuances* of the language. I know no one who unites all these qualifications to the same extent as yourself, and if anything I can say will spur you on, I would urge you to rescue these memorials of a forgotten past, before it is too late. May the success of this your first book lead you on to greater things.

Yours sincerely,

R. B. WOOD.

MALABAR SERIES

WYNAD: ITS PEOPLES AND TRADITIONS

CONTENTS

ILLUSTRATIONS

FRONTISPIECE—*Deputy Collector's Office, Manantoddy.*

PREFACE

WYNAD has always interested me. The inhabitants of the plains have no idea of the several races that have settled in Wynad and of the legends relating to shrines and other places of interest in this taluk. The idea sprung up in my mind that a short account of this country would be interesting and useful, and being encouraged in this idea by Mr. Wood, I.C.S., Collector of Malabar, I availed myself of the opportunity of my stay for two years in Wynad to collect the information which I present to the public in these pages.

I am grateful to Mr. Wood for his kind permission to associate his name with this work and for the complimentary terms in which he has expressed his opinion about the merits of the book.

The ancient history was the most difficult part of the task. No two versions agreed as to what transpired in the days gone by and it was only on securing a copy of the Mackenzie manuscript —recorded in 1810—that I was able to deal with the subject.

The chapter on Political history was compiled from the *Madras Manual of Administration*, the *Malabar Manual* and the *Malabar Gazetteer*, and the extracts from the *Madras Times* and the *Madras Mail* published on pages 1 & 46, as also the reference to the visit of the Governor of Madras on page 4 were taken from *Francis Ford's* pamphlet on "The Wynad and the planting Industry of Southern India."

I have to thank Dr. A. Hewston of Manantoddy and Mr. C. E. Abbott, Meppadi, for details of Planting Industry. The remaining chapters were written from information received from the people of Wynad, the customs and manners of the hill tribes being based on the versions given by the elders of the respective Communities.

My thanks are due to Mr. V. Krishnan of Manantoddy for the photographs. I need hardly add that the Vasanțā Press, Adyar, and Messrs. Venkiah Brothers, Madras, have maintained their reputation for good work.

I have an idea of continuing the Malabar Series and if this, my first attempt is appreciated by the public, I shall endeavour to bring out the second part in the course of another year.

C. GOPALAN NAIR.

Panoramic view from the top of Tamarasseri ghat towards the Arabian Sea, a distance of thirty-nine miles.

"High mountains rise to the left with water glistening on bare black rocks like tears of gladness in the eyes of sorrow; forests stretch away here with gentle slope and easy undulation, there down precipice and steep declivity; far below lie swamps choked with thorny thicket and rank coarse grasses, breeding fevers and miasma, but yet in whose bosoms are stored the streams which water those long stretches of rice fields, here sere and yellow after the sickle of the reaper, there whitening unto harvest or again a vivid green where the second crop matures. Hills everywhere, some arid, red and unfruitful, more covered in the feathery foliage of these Eastern orchards.

Here and there smoke curls up in the still noon-tide air; or the glint of some mosque or temple or riverpool catches the eye. As the distance grows farther, hill and field all merge into one green plain, and beyond gleams the sea, hard to be discerned from the heaven that bends down and meets it. As you gaze, the thought rises from the heart that in such fair and well-ordered beauty, the affairs of this world may perchance appear from the Throne of Heaven with all their inequality, so strange, so little comprehendable by us the dwellers amid its hills and valleys."—MADRAS TIMES.

CHAPTER I

A BIRD'S-EYE VIEW

Wynad, as its name signifies, is the land of forests. The correct name is *Vana-nad* (Forest country) which, by lapse of time, is pronounced Vaya-nad or Wynad, as it is now spelt.

It is a mountainous country, with a general elevation of 2,000 to 4,000 feet and with ranges of hills, some with peaks over 7,000 feet high. To the west and south are the low lands of Malabar, to the east rise the Nilgiri hills, to the north-east lies the Mysore plateau, while to the north-west the chain of ghats stretches away into the province of Coorg.

It is the sanitarium of Malabar from October to the end of February when the climate is dry, cool and salubrious. March,

April and May are the unhealthy months when malarial fever is prevalent. Its fertility is unsurpassed and its scenery is picturesque. When Sir M. E. Grant Duff, Governor of Madras, visited the District, he is said to have asserted that had Wynad been in Europe its fortune would have been made as a pleasure resort: it would be the favourite haunt of the landscape painter and views from it would appear in every picture gallery.

For the sportsman there is game in plenty. Tiger, panther and bear, wild elephant and bison, sambhur, deer and jungle sheep, jungle fowl, spur fowl, pigeons and snipe, all these are in evidence in this country.

According to tradition, Wynad was under the sway of *Vedar* (hunter) kings. These were conquered by the Kottayam and Kurumbranad Rajas who partitioned the country into Wynad and Parakkumeethil. Subsequently the Kottayam Raja, the ruler of Wynad proper, secured the sovereignty of Parakkumeethil also, and the whole country was under his sway when Tippu of Mysore exacted from the senior Raja of

Kottayam a deed of relinquishment of his rights over Wynad in 1786. On the fall of Seringapatam in 1799, Wynad became part of the British Empire. Kerala Varma Raja of Kottayam revolted against the British Power and was killed in 1805, after which peace reigned in the country interrupted only by a small rebellion of Kurichiyars and Kurumbers in 1812. This however, was soon quelled.

In 1877, three of the amsams[1] that formed part of Wynad, *viz.*, Munnanad, Nambalakode and Cherankode, were transferred for administrative purposes to the District of Nilgiris. An enquiry into the jenmam titles to lands in Wynad was commenced in 1884, and four years later, the properties that belonged to Kerala Varma Raja (the Pazhassi rebel) and his adherents were formally declared to belong to Government. In 1889, the settlement of land revenue on modern lines was introduced into Wynad.

Excluding the portion transferred to the Nilgiris, Wynad, as it now exists, covers an area of 821 square miles, and its population

[1] *Amsam*—Group of desams or villages.

according to the census of 1901, was 75,149.

Paddy is the chief wet crop, and ragi the chief dry crop. Rice is the staple food of the inhabitants, ragi being used more by the hill tribes. Cardamoms are grown near Pēria and Koroth on the slopes of the ghats: cocoanut trees and arecanuts do not thrive in the country. Pepper, an indigenous product of North Malabar, was first introduced by the natives of Wynad; subsequently European planters extended its cultivation. To these planters belongs the credit of introducing coffee, cinchona, rubber and tea, and the last named product has taken a firm hold in the country.

The quartz reefs of Wynad are auriferous, and in the seventies, on the existence of gold being widely known, a small company by name Alpha was started under the direction of Mr. Withers from Australia. In 1880, Wynad was the scene of the "wildest, maddest, and grossest speculation" and 33 English companies were floated with an aggregate nominai capital of over four million pounds sterling. The enterprise ended in failure and operations were given up in the course of two to three years. It is still believed that Wynad is rich in gold reefs, but it has been declared by a specialist that with the "methods at present available" gold-mining is not likely to be remunerative.[1]

Wynad has a bright future before it but for the dark spot which threatens to render it unpopular. This is malaria, but it is hoped that by the further clearing of forests and the opening up of lands this will gradually disappear. The opening of railway communication through these forests would induce people from the plains to settle in Wynad and to reclaim the extensive waste lands; this is evidently impracticable and is but a dream.

NOTE—The name Wynad has been derived in different ways:

(1) *Wynad* lit., the open or champaign country.

Bailu (Can.), a field having water suitable for growing rice, a plain.

Nādu (Can.), a division of a district.

(*Grigg's Manual of the Nilgiri District*, page 1.)

---

[1] Since writing the above, an expert mining Engineer has arrived and is engaged in assaying in the neighbourhood of Manantoddy.

(2) *Wynaud* (Upper Country) is, as its name denotes, an elevated plateau.

(*Madras Manual of Administration*, Vol.II. p. 143.)

(3) *Wynaud*, (Vayanatu. Mal.: Wynaud).

From (*Vayal*, Mal.: Open field, *Nātu*, Mal.: country).

Sanskrit name (Mayakshetra), meaning district of Mayan, architect of the deityans.

(*Madras Manual of Administration*, Vol. III. p. 1025.)

I have added a fourth derivation "Vananad" in accordance with the popular belief in this country. This derivation seems more probable, especially as the country is more a land of (*Vana*) forests than of fields.

CHAPTER II

ANCIENT HISTORY

The earliest record of a ruling family in Kerala exists in Wynad in the shape of a rock-inscription in the Edakal cave four miles south-west of Sultan's Battery. The walls of the cave are covered with "rude, fanciful drawings" and one of the inscriptions was suggested by Dr. Hultzch to be "the writing of the glorious Vishnu Varma, the propagator of the Kudumbiyil family". *(Malabar Gazetteer.)* That Kudumbiyil family held sway over Wynad must be accepted as an established fact, but it is impossible to fix the period when they lived and reigned. The author of the *Malabar Gazetteer* writes that "tradition points to a time when a line of Vedar kings held sway and the story goes on to record that an ill-judged capture of a Kshattriya pilgrim to the famous Tirunelli shrine led to the invasion and subjugation of the country by the Kshattriya princes of Kottayam and Kurumbranad." This tradition as recorded by certain leading inhabitants of Wynad on 15th *Vrischikam* 986 M.E. (28th November, 1810), is given below.

The Vedar kings were ruling the country when the Kshattriya ruler of Kumbala (Kumbazha-Kasergode in South Canara) happened to go on a pilgrimage to the Tirunelli temple. He was taken prisoner and carried before the Vedar Raja at the Velikumbam Fort (Veliyambam in Puthadi amsam) and on being pressed to marry a daughter of the Vedar ruling family, he consented on condition that the ceremony should be celebrated in accordance with Kshattriya customs. This was allowed and an auspicious day, a month hence, was fixed for the celebration of the marriage. Meanwhile, the Kumbala Raja communicated with the Rajas of Kottayam and Kurumbranad, who came up with their forces and encamped in the neighbourhood of the Fort. The Kumbala

Raja's attendant, an ascetic with matted hair and an Erati by caste, was entrusted with the duty of beating the drum to commence the festivities; but this was really a signal to commence the onslaught, and on hearing it, the two Rajas with their united forces destroyed the Vedar king; Kumbala Raja was rescued, but he insisted that as he had promised to marry the Vedar girl, he must at least find a substitute and one Nanthillath Nambiar was then prevailed upon to marry her. On this marriage, he was appointed as the ruler of Velikumbam (Veliyambam) with supreme authority over the surviving Vedars. Kumbala Raja having left the country back to go to his own domains, it was decided that Wynad should be partitioned between the Kottayam and Kurumbranad Rajas. The Kottayam Raja left Mathangode and the Kurumbranad Raja left Koliyadi, and it was settled that their meeting place should be the boundary between the two countries. They met at Pazhupathur, and the North-west Wynad known as Wynad proper became the Kottayam Raja's share, and the South-east Wynad known as Parakkumeethil the Kurumbranad Raja's share. For some time they ruled their respective portions, but in consequence of disputes between them, the Kurumbranad Raja gave up his country to the Kottayam Raja, except the palace and some landed properties, and the Kottayam Raja held sway throughout the Wynad including Parakkumeethil.

The Erati ascetic did good service and it was resolved to reward him. The Rajas thought him a lucky man (*Bhāgiyavān*), and in entrusting him with the sovereignty of Muttil, called him the founder of "Bhāgiya Swarupam" (family of good luck) which name has since been abbreviated into "Pakka Swarupam."

The above tradition was handed down from generation to generation, and in 1810, the facts, as above stated, were recorded by certain leading inhabitants of Wynad in pursuance of an order of the Zilla Court of North Malabar, dated 29th Thulam 986 M.E. (12th November, 1810[1]). The tradition has undergone various changes and there is now

[1] *Mackenzie Manuscript.*

hardly any one who could give a correct account of how the Kottayam Rajas became the rulers of Wynad. The record is therefore interesting and shows one of the several stages through which Wynad passed before it became part and parcel of the British Empire. Veliyambam and Pakam families became extinct and their properties were first escheated to the Kottayam Raja and then to the British Government.

Pazhupathur is a place near Sultan's Battery, and Padiri rock on the way from Meenangadi to Battery is pointed out as the exact boundary dividing the respective tracts parcelled out between the two Rajas. The name Parakkumeethil (lit., above the rock), refers to the amsams south-east of that rock and in that portion the Kurumbranad Raja still holds some property including a residence known as Ramangalath Kovilagam.[1]

Arippan and Vedan were the names of the last Vedar rulers. Arippan ruled over the tract lying north of Panamaram, and Aripatta Kunnu in Tavinjal amsam on which his fort

---

[1] *Kovilagam*—Palace.

stood, was called after him. Vedan ruled over the tract lying south of Panamaram river and the *Vedan Kottas* (Vedan forts) in Pakkam and Nenmini amsams were called after him. These rulers are legendary characters but there must be some foundation of truth in the legend, since their names are as familiar to the people of Wynad, as Cheraman Perumal's name is to the inhabitants of the plains.

Mulla Kurumbers are said to belong to Arippan's race and Vettu (or Urali) Kurumbers to Vedan's race. Their claim to this nationality is supported by the following passage in the Madras Journal of Literature and Science (1889): "We are very insufficiently informed about the early history of the Kurumbers. Before they settled down to anything like domestic life they roamed as *Vedas* in the virgin forests hunting the deer for its flesh and the wild animals for their own safety." Dr. Oppert speaks of "*Kudumban*" as identical with "*Kudumbi*" and "*Kurumban*" and it is possible that the Kurumbers were the original inhabitants of Wynad during the reign of the Kudumbiyil family. Evidently these Kurumbers carved out a kingdom for themselves and the Vedar kings Arippan and Vedan, mentioned above, were the last of the line.

CHAPTER III

KOTTAYAM REGIME

Information is meagre as regards the administration of Parakkumeethil under the sway of the Raja of Kurumbranad. But, in respect of Wynad proper, the tract set apart for the Raja of Kottayam, the details of administration, so far as could be ascertained, are given in this chapter.

The Rajas of Kottayam were wise and capable administrators and introduced a settled form of government into the country which became theirs by conquest. It was during their reign that the country was divided into *Nads* (divisions) and placed under Nayar chieftains for purposes of administration, and though the Kottayam family have now no jurisdiction in disputes falling under the criminal law, they still exercise their authority in social matters. Wynad proper was under the sway of the Western branch of the Kottayam family until the death of Pazhassi Raja in 1805; and since then the senior Raja of *Kizhekke Kovilagam* (Eastern palace) is the final appellate authority in all social questions.

The capital selected by the Rajas of Kottayam is the station now known as Manantoddy which is an abbreviation of *Maha-Ananda-Vati*, meaning "Garden of delight." It is no exaggeration to say that no more appropriate name could have been conceived. As the healthiest station in Wynad, as an open country in the midst of forests, with a beautiful stream running by, with a cool and salubrious climate and an up-to-date bazaar, it is still a "garden of delight," to the inhabitants of Wynad and to those in the plains who desire rest, peace and a cool climate after their experiences in the low country.

At this station, at Kazhukottur in Tavinjal amsam, and at Mathangode in Kuppathode, the Raja built palaces and shrines, and though the palaces are now no more, having collapsed by time and by neglect, the shrines exist and are kept up though not in the same grand style as before. In one of these shrines (Theythal Bhagavathi shrine), the officiating priest even now places a burning lamp and flowers in the Raja's seat of honour, as doing homage to the ruler who during his reign used to attend the annual festival.

The name of Kazhukottur is connected with "Kazhu"—gallows—where gallows were erected to hang criminals.

As already stated Wynad proper or North-west Wynad was divided into *Nads* or smaller divisions and placed under Nayar chieftains for purposes of administration.

1. Muthornad (Muthakur-nad, country of the eldest). This division was placed under the direct control of the senior Raja.

The villages included in this division are: Pēria, Tavinjal and Edavaka, and the following families were appointed as chieftains over them:

(1) Vazhathattil Nayar.
(2) Tavinjal Nayar.
(3) Mulliyankizhil Nayar.

(4) Alattil Nayar.
(5) Ayiravittil Nayar.
(6) Varayal Nayar.

These six are jointly known as "Aruvarambath Jenmakkars." (Landlords of six boundaries.)

2. Ellornad (Elankur-nad, Nad of the younger branch). This was placed under the direct control of the second Raja.

This consists of Vemom and Tirunelli amsams.

Chieftains: (1) Edachana Nayar.
(2) Vemom Nambiar.

They are known as "Karushor" (*Kariya Purushanmar*), men who administer the affairs of "Elankuttil Swarupam."

3. Wynad; 4. Porunnanur and 5. Nallurnad were placed under the third Raja.

Wynad comprises Kuppathode, Purakkadi, Anjukunnu and Puthadi amsams.

Chieftains: (1) Kuppathode Nayar.
(2) Tonder Nambiar.
(3) Pulpadi Nayar.
(4) Chikkalur Nayar.

These constitute "Wynad Swarupam."

4. Porunnanur comprising Porunnanur and Vellamunda amsams.

Chieftains: (1) Manchan Nambiar.
(2) Karingari Nayar.
(3) Mangalasseri Nayar.
(4) Vattathode Nambiar
(5) Cherukara Nayar.

known as "Porunnanur Swarupam."

5. Nallurnad consisting of the amsam of that name.

The Chieftains are:—

(1) Manchan Nambiar.
(2) Karingari Nayar.
(3) Edachana Nayar.

6. Kurumbala Nad comprising Kurumbala and Kottathara amsams.

This division was placed under Avinjat Nayar of Payyormala, Kurumbranad Taluk. He was the son of the Kottayam Raja, who gave him the title of "Vazhunnavar" (Ruler). Two Nayars—Thenamangalath Nayar, Poyil Nayar—were appointed as local Chieftains. Avinjat family was subsequently divided into Avinjat and Kuthali, and the senior members of these families hold the position of Vazhunnavars in Kurumbala and Kottathara respectively.

7. Edanataskur, comprising amsams of Kottapadi, Kalpetta and Vayitri with (1) Kalpetta Nayar and (2) Kanthamangalath Nayar, as chieftains.

8. Tondernad consisting of the amsam of that name was placed under Nelliote Thirumulpad, who granted it to his son Thonder Nambiar, the senior Nambiar being styled "Kovil" and his residence "Mel kotta" (Upper Fort).

9. Muttil and Pakkam Desams[1] were under "Bhagiam or Pakam Swarupam" and

10. Veliyambam under the Veliyambam Vazhunnavar (Ruler), as already stated in Chapter II.

Administration

The administration of the country was in the hands of chieftains. When caste rules are violated the chieftains generally recommend *Prāyaschittham* (expiatory observance), and a member of the offender's family is sent to

[1] *Desam*—Village.

pay homage to the senior Raja of Kottayam. He presents the *Neyyamirta* (offerings) in the shape of money. A wealthy family presents 64 fanams, a middle class family 32 fanams, and a poor one 16 fanams (fanam=4 As.). On the fine being placed in a *kindi* (brass vessel) in the Raja's presence, he asks the party to see the *unnis* (children) and the mother, thereby meaning the second and third Rajas, and the *Valiya Thamburatti* (senior princess). The party concerned makes presents to them on a smaller scale. On orders (*tharaku*) being then sent from the palace, the offender is admitted to caste on *Prāyaschittham* to the deity of his *Nād*, which is done by a big feast, and payments ranging from 16 to 64 fanams as a fine, which goes to the temple fund.

Whenever there is a *Pallikettu* (Marriage) ceremony in the Raja's family or when the senior Raja or Thamburatti dies, intimation is given to the chieftains, who respond by going to the Kovilagam (palace) and making presents. These old customs are still continued.

Criminal and Civil Jurisdiction

This was also in the hands of the Nayar chieftains. On complaints being made, the chieftains meet at the house of the senior member and decide the case, which, if it ends in conviction, is followed by a fine to the deity. If it so happens that any complaint is pending at the time of the annual festival of the temple it would be decided there. Before the festival begins, the question is put by the senior chieftain "Are there any disputes in the country?[1]" The parties interested step forward, their cases are heard and disposed of in the presence of the deity by the chieftains and the elders of the country before the festival commences. This system of Panchayet was well adapted to the state of the country with all the acts ratified by the presence of the deity, before whom no falsehood would be uttered. Swearing is now done as a matter of course in the courts of law without feeling any corresponding obligation to speak the truth, but the presence of the deity and the invocation by the people

[1] "*Nāttu Vazhakkangal Vallathum Undō?*" Mal.

to help them tended towards a satisfactory decision being arrived at in the days gone by.

The system of administration adopted, deserves encomium. No one chieftain was allowed to exercise any independent power and every dispute had to be heard and disposed of by the assembly of chieftains. The Raja had to address them jointly in matters affecting the *Nād* and even now, when a representation is made about caste customs, the report is submitted by the chieftains jointly and the *Tharaku* (order) is also addressed to the corporate body, (such as "Aruvarambath Jenmakkars," "Elankuttil Swarupam," etc.), instead of to individual chieftains.

Royal Prerogative

The right of escheat is not new to the present Government: the Kottayam Raja also had exercised it. The right of *Ezha*, *Kozha*, *Thappu-Pizha*, vested in the ruler.

Ezha—Property of persons dying without heirs.

Kozha—Fine imposed, in addition to expiatory observances, for violation of caste customs.

Thappu-Pizha—Fine for offences committed.

The population consisted of Hindus and they were evidently happy under the reign of the Kottayam family. This happy state of things was disturbed by the aggressions of the Muhammadans from Mysore, and the unsettled state consequent on the Mysore invasion continued until the fall of Seringapatam in 1799 and the cession of Wynad to the British Government.

CHAPTER IV

POLITICAL HISTORY

Wynad stands unique in its political history. This was the only taluk in Malabar which never bowed its neck to the Mysore yoke and which defied the British power until its ruler fell, fighting against the troops of the East India Company. This ruler was the Kerala Varma Raja of Pazhassi Kovilagam (Pazhassi palace) of Kottayam dynasty and his history is practically the political history of Wynad from 1786 to 30th November, 1805.

Hyder Ali's hordes were devastating Malabar in 1766 and the rulers of Kottayam had fled for safety to Travancore where the child Kerala Varma was living with his relations. Wynad remained undisturbed until 1773, when a Mysorean army passed through the country by the Tamarasseri ghat on its way to Calicut.

In 1780 on the outbreak of the second Mysore War, Ravi Varma the senior Raja, returned from Travancore with his nephew Kerala Varma and assisted the beleaguered English factors at the seige of Tellicherry with an army of 2,000 Nayars, and in 1786 when Ravi Varma visited Tippu Sultan in Coorg, he—the Sultan—exacted from him a deed of relinquishment of all his rights over Wynad.

The Kottayam family had then three branches:

1. *Kizhekke Kovilagam*—Eastern Palace.
2. *Patinhare Kovilagam*—Western Palace.
3. *Thekke Kovilagam*—Southern Palace.

Wynad was under the sovereignty of the Western branch of which Kerala Varma was the head. He resented the action of the senior Raja and refused to submit to the Mysoreans with whom he was engaged in desultory warfare from 1787 to the beginning of the Third Mysore War in 1790. On 4th May of that year, Robert Taylor, chief of the English settlement at Tellicherry granted a cowle to Kerala Varma Raja that the English East India Company would assist and protect him and do every thing in their power to render him independent of Tippu if he would enter heartily into the war against the Sultan. The war was waged, and under the treaty of peace dated 18th March, 1792, Malabar was ceded to the Company by the Sultan of Mysore.

It was a disputed point whether Wynad was included in this cession and it was not decided until the arrival of Lord Mornington in India in 1798, when it was finally settled that Wynad had remained part of Tippu's dominions.

As soon as the treaty of Seringapatam was signed in 1792, the East India Company appointed Joint Commissioners for the administration of Malabar. They committed the initial mistake of entrusting Kottayam to the Kurumbranad Raja, who had no influence in the country, and Kerala Varma Raja, who was all-powerful in Kottayam, promptly showed his contempt for both the alleged authority of his uncle the Kurumbranad Raja and the regulations of the East

India Company by stopping all collections of revenue in the district and by taking the law in his own hands against erring Moplas.

Efforts were made by the Company to surprise the Raja in his palace at Pazhassi, in Kottayam Taluk, but the Raja had a secure retreat in the wilds of Wynad. The troops sent against him were hampered by difficulties of transport and lack of supplies, and a series of minor reverses culminated on March 18, 1797, in a detachment of 1,100 men being cut to pieces in the Pēria pass. The Governor of Bombay and the Commander-in-Chief visited Malabar to investigate the state of the District and cancelled the agreement with the Kurumbranad Raja; peace was restored through the good offices of the Chirakkal Raja, Kerala Varma being paid Rs. 8,000 a year as pension.

In 1799, after the fall of Seringapatam, Wynad had been ceded to the British but Kerala Varma Raja resisted all attempts of the Company to take possession of the country and persevered in hostilities until 1805. On November 30th of that year, Mr. Baber,

Sub-Collector of North Malabar Division surprised him in his retreat in the neighbourhood of the Pulpalli forest and had the "infinite satisfaction" of reporting to Government that he had "the good fortune to come up with the Cotiote Kerala Varma Raja *alias* the Pyche Raja and with the assistance of Captain Clapham and 50 Sepoys and 100 Kolkars[1] to chastise this rebel chieftain by destroying him and five of his followers." The rebellion died a natural death afterwards.

The following extract from Mr. Baber's letter[2] dated 31st December, 1805, to the Collector of Malabar explains the events immediately preceding the Raja's death and contains the writer's views as regards the Raja's character. To the student of Wynad history it is interesting reading.

"Having said this much of the plan of operations that had been adopted, I now come to those which terminated the career of the Pyche (Palassi) chieftain."

"I before said that one of my objects by getting in the inhabitants of Pulpally

---

[1] *Kolkars*—Peons. [2] *Malabar Manual.*

(Pulpalli) was to obtain accurate information of the rebels. This I did not think prudent to commence upon too early lest they should take the alarm. I preferred trying all my persuasive means to gain their confidence and to wean them from their connections. For this purpose I had them before me and took every opportunity of representing the folly of countenancing a body of men so truly contemptible, and who had no other end than to involve them in one common ruin. I pointed to them in the strongest colours the power and lenity of the British Government, and at last, what with exhortation and occasional presents, had succeeded in inducing several of these, who had been of most essential service to the Raja's party, to send their Paṇiyars (*Paṇiyar*—agricultural labourers) out in quest of information. I took the precaution of swearing all whom I employed to secrecy. With many agents, I could not fail of success in some one of them. On the 30th ultimo, three of them at last brought me intelligence of the Pyche (Palassi) Raja and all the rebel leaders, with the exception of Palora Jamen (Pallur Eman) being then in the opposite side of the Kangara river, a short distance in Mysore, and this so unequivocally that I determined to act upon it. I accordingly requested of Lieutenant-Colonel Hill to assist me with 50 Sepoys and an Officer, with which force and about 100 kolkars, half Captain Watson's Police, half my own locals, I marched at nine o'clock at night; and such was the secrecy in which we set off that our guides even did not know my intention until the moment we took our departure. Previous to this I had deemed it expedient to make a feint to divert the attention of the rebels (who I thought it probable might have their spies in camp) by detaching 70 of my kolkars, under the Sheristadar, under the pretext of going in pursuit of Palora Jamen who was reported to be in the Komanpany Mala in the South-eastern direction, while they had secret instructions after marching half-way to this mountain to strike off eastward to the Kallir Mountain and there lie in ambush near to paths to cut off the retreat of any fugitives who would, in most probability, go off in that direction in the event of our party coming up with the rebels.

"Such was the nature of the country that although we kept marching the whole night we did not reach the Kangara river until seven the following morning. Here we divided ourselves into two parties, and proceeding along the banks, observed a vast number of huts, all of them bearing every appearance of recent habitation : we continued marching until nine o'clock, when the detachment being fatigued, a halt was proposed. We accordingly halted, and having taken some refreshment, we again started, with the determination of tracing every jungly path: so fully pursuaded was I, as well from the earnestness of our guides as the consideration that this was a part of Mysore that our troops had at no time penetrated or perhaps even thought of doing, that the rebels must be concealed in some parts of these jungles. After proceeding about a mile and a half through very high grass and thick teak forests into the Mysore country, Charen Subedar of Captain Watson's armed police, who was leading the advanced party suddenly halted and beckonning to me, told me he heard voices. I immediately ran to the spot, and having advanced a few steps, I saw distinctly to the left about ten persons, unsuspecting of danger, on the banks of the Mavila Toda, or Nulla to our left. Although Captain Clapham and the sepoys as well as the greater part of the kolkars, were in the rear, I still deemed it prudent to proceed, apprehensive lest we should be discovered and all hopes of surprise thereby frustrated. I accordingly ordered the advance, which consisted of about thirty men, to dash on, which they accordingly did with great gallantry, with Charen Subedar at their head. In a moment the advance was in the midst of the enemy, fighting most bravely. The contest was but of short duration. Several of the rebels had fallen, whom the kolkars were despatching, and a running fight was kept up after the rest till we could see no more of them. Just at this time a firing was heard to the right;

we accordingly returned, when we saw the sepoys and kolkars engaged with a fresh body of rebels, who proved to be of Coongan's (Kungan's) party, but who fled after a few shots had been fired at them and though pursued, were seen nothing more of. From one of the rebels of the first party to the left, whom I discovered concealed in the grass, I learnt that the Pyche (Palassi) Raja was amongst those whom we first observed on the banks of the Nulla, and it was only on my return from the pursuit that I learnt that the Raja was amongst the first who had fallen. It fell to the lot of one of my Cutcherry servants, Canara Menon, to arrest the flight of the Raja, which he did at the hazard of his life (the Raja having put his musket to his breast) and it is worthy of mention that this extraordinary personage, though in the moment of death, called out in the most dignified and commanding manner to the Menon, "Not to approach and defile his person". Aralat Cootty Nambiar, the only one remaining of those rebels proscribed by Colonel Stevenson and a most faithful adherent of the Raja made a most desperate resistance, but at last fell over-powered by the superior skill of one of the parbutties (pravritti) in Wynad; four other followers of the Raja were also killed, two taken prisoners together with the Raja's lady and several female attendants. There was no other property discovered, but a gold Cuttaram (Katharam or Kattaram—dagger) or knife and a waist-chain; the former I have now in my possession, the latter I presented to Captain Clapham. And from the accounts of the Raja's lady, they had been reduced to the greatest distresses in particular for the last ten days. The Raja's body was taken up and put into my palanquin, while the lady who was dreadfully reduced from sickness was put into Captain Clapham's. Finding any further pursuit of the rebel useless, we made a disposition of our forces and returned to Chomady which we reached about six in the afternoon without having met with any further occurrences on the road. The following day the Raja's body was despatched under a strong escort to

Manantoddy, and the Sheristadar sent with it with orders to assemble all the Brahmins and to see that the customary honours were performed at his funeral. I was induced to this conduct from the consideration that although a rebel, he was one of the natural chieftains of the country, and might be considered on that account rather as a fallen enemy. If I have acted injudiciously, I hope some allowances will be made for my feelings on such an occasion.

"Thus terminated the career of a man who has been enabled to persevere in hostilities against the Company for nearly nine years, during which many thousand valuable lives have been sacrificed and sums of money beyond all calculation expended.

"Notwithstanding that every effort of moderation and lenity was pursued towards the Raja, nothing could get the better of his natural restlessness and ferocity of disposition, which, aided by the evil counsels of his advisers, impelled him to the most desperate acts and produced an infatuation which rendered him insensible to the dictates of humanity or reason. His annihilation became necessary for the stability and security of the Government and its subjects. While this severe necessity existed, the recollection of the services he has performed during the infancy of our Government cannot but inspire us with a sentiment of regret that a man so formed should have pursued a conduct that should have thrown so insuperable a bar to all kinds of accommodations. To temporise further than was done would have been to yield, and to have yielded would have afforded a precedent which might have been fatal to the British Government in India.

"But it will not be necessary for me to enlarge to you who are so well acquainted with this chieftain's history, on the leading features of so extraordinary and singular a character. The records in England and India will convey to posterity a just idea of him."

Mr. Baber admired the great qualities of the Raja and remarked that the inhabitants entertained towards the Raja "a regard and respect bordering on veneration which not even his death can efface." These words were prophetic; more than a century has passed and his name is still cherished by the people as the Saktan[1] Raja.

---

[1] *Saktan*—Powerful: Great.

CHAPTER V

THE PLANTING INDUSTRY

Coffee. In the first half of the nineteenth century Manantoddy was a military station and the troops were cantoned on the hill on which the Travellers' Bungalow now stands. This bungalow was the mess house of the officers of the detachment. The Officer in command appears to have planted coffee experimentally on this hill employing his men for the work, and the tree flourished on this fertile soil. In 1820 or thereabouts, a partner of Messrs. Parry & Co., was on his way from Madras, across the peninsula to Calicut, and went up the Kuttiyadi ghat on a visit to their coffee estates on the Baba Budan Hills in Northern Mysore. He stopped with the officers of the detachment and in course of conversation, when the visitor remarked on the difficulties of travel to the distant coffee estates, one of the officers pointed out to him the flourishing coffee plants on the Manantoddy hill just behind the mess. He was greatly impressed with the growth of the trees and the quantity of the crop, and on his return to Madras sent Mr. King to purchase Grass hills near Manantoddy and experiment on coffee cultivation. He built a bungalow on the hill near Manantoddy Ferry and opened about 75 acres of land for coffee. This was the first attempt, which however ended in failure. Mr. Pugh from Ceylon, an experienced planter then visited Manantoddy and established the first coffee estate known as the Pew estate. The exact year is not known, but it was between 1830 and 1840. North Wynad then became a planting centre with all the paraphernalia of a European club and a race course. Coffee was at its best between 1860

NOTE—There is another version that it was Major Glasson who opened the first Coffee Estate in Manantoddy in 1840. The account given here was furnished by Dr. Hewston, an old resident of Manantoddy.

and 1875 and it was in 1870 that leaf disease first appeared. This was the chief cause of the decline of the industry, though borer and the introduction of the Ceylon system of planting without shade did a lot of harm. The industry was thus ruined and the planter had recourse to cinchona. The first cinchonas were planted in Cherampadi by Captain Cox and Mr. Irvine in 1868 as an avenue, but it was not until the early seventies that the industry was started to any great extent with *Cinchona Succirubra*. Ledgers (i.e., *Cinchona Ledgereana*) followed some ten years later, and from 1880 to 1890 it was largely grown, but the immense exports from Ceylon and later from Java sent the price down to what would hardly pay for the harvesting and shipping, let alone any question of return on the capital or of cultivation charges. This is an instance of an industry being ruined by over-production. Before the Ceylon exports began to be felt (say about 1880) the price of quinine was £1 per ounce but in the beginning of the nineties, it went down to ten pence and now the wholesale price is less than a shilling. There is very little cinchona now remaining in Wynad.

Tea began to be planted on various estates in Wynad from 1892 forward. It had existed before then on Perindotty which Messrs. Parry & Co., had worked for years as a tea estate. On the failure of coffee and cinchona many estates were planted with tea and as prices have risen extensions have gone on. It does very well in Wynad and the total output as reported in official returns is given below:

Year		*Acreage*		*Manufactured Tea*
1907	...	4,531	...	1,749,062 lbs.
1908	...	4,686	...	1,751,526 ,,
1909	...	5,078	...	2,283,429 ,,

Tea is now confined to South Wynad; but lands are now being taken up for tea planting also in North Wynad, which in course of time, will recover its past glory, with the many advantages incidental to the introduction of this valuable industry into this at present deserted part of Wynad. The technical names found on the labels of tea packets are the names of each of the leaves of the shoot of the tea plant. The bud at the extreme end is the tip or the "Flowery pekoe," the two next "Orange pekoe," the two next "Souchong," and the next two "Congou"

Pepper flourished in North Malabar, and on the failure of coffee, the planters tried it in Wynad. It was first grown there in the sixties and Mr. Powell took charge of a South Wynad Estate with bearing pepper on it in 1875. For some years, it throve, and the disease that is doing so much damage first attracted attention in 1900. Since tea has turned out successful, pepper is merely tolerated by the planter and not encouraged.

Rubber. Ceara rubber was planted experimentally a good many years ago. In 1889 there were full grown trees in Cherambadi and it was then thought that it would not yield any latex in Wynad. No one thought of doing anything with it until 1903 when an expert deputed by the Government made experiments and demonstrated that the trees would yield rubber. In 1904

Mr. C. E. Abbott tapped a number of trees in Moovatee and Poothram Shola Estates near Vayitri (South Wynad). Getting a fair yield he made an experimental shipment, which sold for six shillings per pound. Tapping experiments were made in Rasselas and certain other estates when it was abundantly proved that latex existed in the trees. But the method of tapping then recommended was an unsound one, and so many trees died under the process that it was discontinued. A new method has been since discovered giving good results, and it is proposed to plant Ceara extensively. It grows freely but must be protected from wind.

Para Rubber (*Havea Brazileinsis*) is also being planted on some estates and though the growth is slower than in the low country it does well when carefully planted and cultivated.

Rubber now attracts considerable attention among the planters; but its importance is second only to that of tea.

"The Planter has brought into cultivation land which but for him would have been unproductive at the present day;

he has tilled the desolate mountain-tops; he has turned the hill fastnesses into fruitful gardens; he has made the fever-poisoned valleys to rejoice in health and plenty. By his labours, and at no mean expenditure of British lives and British gold, tracts of jungle which half a century ago gave but a scanty gleaning of gall-nuts and wild honey, to-day produce harvests worth over a million and a half of money."

The above published in the *Madras Mail*, fifteen years ago, sums up the situation admirably. European enterprise has contributed materially to the prosperity of the country and the planting industry is giving work to hundreds of labourers, who in these days of over-population, would otherwise be starving. The country is being opened up year by year and the millions of English money spent here will not be in vain.

CHAPTER VI

PEOPLE OF WYNAD

(*a*) *Chettis.*

1. Edanadan Chettis.
2. Wynadan Chettis.
3. Mandatan Chettis.

(*b*) *Hill tribes.*

1. Kurichiyans.
2. Mullakurumbers.
3. Urali or Vettu Kurumbers
4. Kunduvatiyans.
5. Karimpalans.
6. Kaders.
7. Pathiyans.
8. Uridavans.
9. Thachanad Muppens.
10. Kanaladis.

(*c*) *Aborigines*—Predial slaves.

1. Adiyans.
2. Paniyars.
3. Pulayans.

(*d*) *Aborigines*—Forest dwellers.

4. Jain or Thēn Kurumbers.

5. Kattu Nāykans.

This chapter contains a description of the customs and manners of those peculiar tribes whose ancestors having found their way into Wynad centuries ago, settled here at different times and in different colonies, every community being distinct from the other in customs and manners, language and faith, dress and appearance. These have no kith or kin outside Wynad and the adjoining tracts.

These communities not being correlative to one another, it is difficult to classify them. An attempt is however made, though it may not be very satisfactory.

The Chettis. The three Chettis are by their status and wealth, placed on the top of the list. They are landlords and cultivators, have Brahmin priests to officiate, and have advanced in civilisation to the extent of supplying two members to the Taluk Board of Wynad, one from Edanadan and the other from Wynadân Chetty community.

(1) Kurichiyans, (2) Mullakurumbers,

(3) Urali or Vettu Kurumbers, (4) Kunduvatiyans, (5) Karimpalans, (6) Kaders, (7) Pathiyans, (8) Uridavans, (9) Thachanad Muppens, and (10) Kanaladis may be grouped together as hill tribes, it being impossible to draw any distinction between them, except so far as Kurichiyans are concerned, who admittedly hold the highest position among them.

The next group consists of the predial slaves: (1) Adiyans, (2) Paniyars, (3) Pulayans, and the forest dwellers, (4) Jain or Thēn Kurumbers and (5) Kattu Nāykans. These are the aborigines. About the Paniyars it is stated in the *Imperial Gazetteer* (Vol. I) that they are the most characteristic representatives of the Dravadian type, being probably the "original type of the population of India now modified to a varying extent by the admixture of Aryan, Scythian and Mongoloid elements" Another theory is that the Paniyars are the descendants of the Negroes brought from Zanzibar by Moors trading with the Malabar Coast, and a third theory and the most interesting one is that there existed a "submerged continent of Lemuria extending from Madagascar to the Malay Archipelago linking India with Africa on the one side and with Australia on the other;"[1] a theory which points to an affinity between the aborigines of Australia, the Negroes of Africa and the aborigines of Southern India. On this I am not qualified to comment.

Besides the above hill tribes, there are other inhabitants such as Nayars, Brahmins, Jains, Moplas and Rowthens who have settled in Wynad. They do not really belong to this country, but are descendants of settlers from other places and keep up communication with their ancestral homes, intermarrying among their caste people in their own countries. The Nayars from the plains were the first to come in. They were brought by the Kottayam Raja and were allowed lands to settle on, the leaders among them being appointed to responsible positions as detailed in Chapter III. The Brahmins were brought from the Chola country after the conquest, and they settled in Nallurnad amsam. There are landlords, officials and money-

---

Imperial Gazetteer.

lenders among them and the majority are in well-to-do circumstances. The Jains consisting of Gowdas and Taragans migrated from Mysore for purposes of trade. The title Taragan is not prevalent in Mysore, but was adopted in Wynad by those Jains who settled here under "Taraku" (Royal mandate) of the Kottayam Raja. The Moplas came in from Tellicherry, Kurumbranad and Calicut after the Mysore invasion, and Rowthens have a colony in Kariyampathi (between Kaniambetta and Meenangadi) and are cultivators and tradesmen. Their ancestors hailed from Pudunagaram in Palghat, where they are to be found in large numbers. The history of the above classes properly belongs to the countries from which their ancestors migrated and is therefore not given here.

Edanadan Chettis

This class of Chettis, whose ancestors migrated from Coorg—from a place known as Edanad—have settled in Tirunelli and Puthadi amsams. Where Edanad is and whether there is a place known as Edanad, the present generation of Chettis have no idea. They did not change their customs nor their law of inheritance—the only change in them being in point of dress—whereas they wore the ordinary Chettis' dress in their ancestral home, they now wear the Malayali Mundu (cloth) like the Malabar Nayars. There is no information as to when they migrated.

Agriculturists they are by profession, and the fertile soil of Tirunelli responds to their labours. Their language they claim to be Canarese; but in their own houses they speak a hybrid between Canarese and Malayalam. They are generally illiterate and the few who profess to read and write do so in Malayalam and this is not surprising as Malayalam is the language of the country. In point of religion they are divided into Saivites and Vaishnavites, the former bearing the ash marks on the forehead and the latter the Iyengar mark (Vaishnava), both sects being curiously enough served by a Vaishnavite Vaidika (religious preceptor). This Vaidika is an Iyengar Brahmin of Punnat (southern part of Mysore) and it is rather a mystery how such a Brahmin

EDANADAN CHETTIS.

happened to be the priest of these Chettis. He is the judge or rather arbitrator in questions of religious and social customs; in cases of violation of any caste customs, it is he who decides whether the offender should be outcasted and what Prayaschitham (Penance) should be observed before he could be admitted to the caste privileges. These Chettis have no temples or religious institutions of their own; and recognise the local temples for purpose of worship irrespective of the particular deity who presides.

Makkathayam (succession from father to son) is the law of inheritance observed by this community and their marriage customs deserve notice. Between the bridegroom's and bride's relations, the marriage is settled: and on the day fixed, the bride's party move to the bridegroom's house where after a bath they sit in a pandal erected for the purpose when the bridegroom's father (or in his absence his uncle) pays the bride's parents ten fanams (Rs. 2-8-0) and garlands, after being sanctified by a Brahmin, are exchanged between the bride and the bridegroom. It is rather curious that the garlands should cost 16 fanams (Rs. 4-0-0) while the bride's price is only (Rs. 2-8-0) but yet that is the custom. The feasting continues till the third day when the marriage ceremony closes.

On the husband's death the widow is entitled to be maintained by his relatives but a convenient alternative exists by which if either party wishes she could leave the house on her being paid Rs. 5 and a new cloth, when she could go to her father's, forfeiting her right to her husband's property. She may also take another husband, but not in the manner she was first married. A second marriage is not a legal one and does not convey to her or her children any right to her husband's property and it is merely a Podamuri, as is customary in Malabar, the bride's price being reduced to 5 fanams (Re. 1-4-0) and the garlanding being dispensed with.

Evidently these people have both the real *Makkathayam* marriage and the *Marumakkathayam Sambandham* called Podamuri. The former they retain as a relic of their ancestral custom by which the wife and children suc-

WYNADAN CHETTIS.

ceed to the father's property and the latter they adopted by association with Malayalis whereby the wife and children have no right to the father's property.

These Chettis observe death pollution for 5 to 11 days but beyond a feast during that period and the sprinkling of holy water (Punniaham) from the hands of a Brahmin there is no objection to others mixing with them, touching them or dining with them. They bury or cremate their dead according as is most convenient for the surviving relatives.

The Chettis take meals prepared by Nayars and the milk and ghee presented by them are accepted by Brahmins.

Thus a class of people from Coorg exist in Wynad cultivating the fertile soil of Tirunelli, following their ancestral customs and manners slightly changed by the customs of their adopted country with no relatives beyond the villages where they are now settled and where as agriculturists they live a happy and contented life.

Wynadan Chettis

This is a peculiar class of Chettis, who are found in the four amsams of Kidanganad, Nenmini, Nulpuzha and Muppainad. They are agriculturists by profession, follow the *Marumakkathayam* (succession in mother's line) law like the Nayars have access to the temples in Wynad unlike other Chettis, and the milk and ghee offered by them are accepted by Brahmins and Nayars. Their language is Malayalam: they have the *Achara Kalliyanam*, a substitute for the Malayalam *Sambandham*[1] and they are, when compared to the Chettis of other denominations hailing from the east coast, a favoured class enjoying the privileges of Nayars, excepting in the matter of shaving and washing for which no separate class was assigned to their community and in consequence of which they do it among themselves.

Their ancestors hailed from Dharapuram in Coimbatore and were Vellala Chettis, who for some reason, not clearly ascertainable, left their country, passed through Satyamangalam in Coimbatore, through Melpotta in Mysore, Ponkuli in Nulpuzha (Wynad) and encamped in Ganapathivattam (Sultan's Battery) within a distance of six miles from Thirumangalath

[1] *Sambandham*—Malabar form of marriage.

Kotta (Nenmini Amsam) wherein lived the Raja of Kottayam. As a wise ruler, he induced them to settle down in his country and offered them lands to cultivate. They were about 300 families, and while they had to make certain changes in their appearance—removal of the back tuft of hair to the front, and change of dress from the Tamilian coloured clothing to the Malayali white—they were happy and contented with the privileges of Nayars conferred upon them. Between them and these Chettis there is no touch-pollution.

There is however a slight difference in their marriage customs. The *Achara Kalliyanam*,[1] referred to above, does not permit of the wife living with the husband at his house, and there is therefore a *Mala Kalliyanam*, when the bride and the bridegroom garland (*Mala*) each other, the garland being given by a Brahmin, and the wife gets the right of living with the husband. One who has performed only the less important *Kalliyanam* may remarry in the more respectable form, with the conse-

[1] *Kalliyanam*—Marriage.

quential privilege of the wife and children living in the husband's house.

The Chettis are exclusively agriculturists cultivating wet lands, and also raising dry crops. The Raja appointed as heads of the community the senior members of the following five families:

1. Chiran Chetti in Nenmini.
2. Thomat Chetti in Muppainad.
3. Kollapalli Chetti in Munnanad.
4. Chethalayath Chetti in Chenad desam.
5. Peruvangote Chetti in Kidanganad desam. Their descendants are still recognised as heads of the community in all social functions.

They are bold shikaris and their pastime is the tiger hunt. Their deity *Manmathan* presides over their destinies, with other minor gods and goddesses, one of whom is known as Mudianpuli at the shrine on Edakal Mala. The majority are illiterate but they are now sending their children to school. They are law-abiding and peaceful citizens living on the produce of their lands, but are improvident and always indebted to the clever Mopla money-lender

MANDATAN CHETTIS.

of Sultan's Battery and are unfortunately addicted to drink.

Under the wise administration of the Kottayam Raja they lived and flourished in this wilderness, forgetting their ancestral home, their mother-tongue, and with a system of inheritance different from what prevails among their caste men in Coimbatore.

Mandatan Chettis

About forty families of Mandatan Chettis are to be found in Veliyambam and Pulpalli desams in Puthadi amsam.

They are found nowhere else in Wynad and they appear to have migrated from Gudalur Division of the Nilgiri District where, it is said, about 500 families of this community exist.

Between Mandatan Chettis and Wynadan Chettis, already mentioned, there is a similarity that both bear the *kuduma* in front and the males interdine: but the former follow *Makkathayam* and the latter *Marumakkathayam.*

They have their own paddy and hill cultivation and while they do not go out as labourers, they manage to live on the proceeds of their own cultivation.

They have no separate shrine for their God who is called "Athiralan," and who is worshipped in every house, and any special offering they desire to make is made at Nambulakotta in Gudalur (Nilgiri District) once a year. Marriage is permissible before or after puberty. Arrangements are made by the bridegroom's father or uncle and on the day fixed for the wedding, the father and, in his absence, the paternal uncle or elder brother proceeds to the bride's house with *thali* and ear ornaments, which are handed over to the father of the bride. She wears them and accompanies the party to the bridegroom's home. The ceremony lasts generally for five days and the garlanding is done on the third day in a special pandal erected for the occasion, where the bridegroom ties the *thali* round the neck of the bride and they exchange garlands which, for a consideration of a rupee and eight annas, a Brahmin provides.

Cremation is the rule among them except where children die, but in cases of death from cholera and small-pox, the dead are buried and not cremated. Fifteen days'

KURICHIYANS.

pollution is observed after death.

The husband may divorce the wife and the latter may marry again, but the children live with the father. On the husbands' death, his brother may marry the widow; in fact it is the brother's right to marry her to the exclusion of a stranger.

The origin of these Chettis cannot be ascertained. They have adopted the *kuduma* in front which is a Malabar custom: but everything else indicates their origin as from outside Malabar. Their headquarters, as they represent, is in the Gudalur Division of the Nilgiri District, but their original home is unknown.

KURICHIYANS

The name Kurichiyan was given by the Kottayam Raja to this class of people as they were adepts in archery. The expression is "Kuri-vechavan," (he who took aim). Another derivation is suggested in the *Gazetteer* from Kurichchi—hill country. They belonged to a class of Nayars known as "Theke Kari Nayar" meaning Karinayar of south, indicating Venad or Travancore. Whether they exist still in Travancore, there is no information.

The traditionary account of the Kurichiyans' advent into this country is that the Kottayam Raja brought them for fighting the Vedar rulers Arippen and Vedan. Their castemen would not take them back and they settled in Wynad and in the hilly parts of Kottayam. The number of families so settled is said to be 148.

Their houses are called "Mittam," and while recognising the gods of the Nayars of this country, their own special deity is "Malakari" an aspect of Siva as a hunter, and in every mittam a place is allotted for smaller local deities also. Offering to the deities is given after the harvest in either of the two methods "Thera" or "Koll". For the Thera, the platform or shrine where the *puja* (worship) is to be performed is purified by holy water from a Brahmin's hands, and a Kurichiyan dressed up for the occasion, with a white head-dress, acts as an oracle. The *Kumbham-Vettal* (cutting the vessel) then takes place, the Muppen—headman—cutting a bamboo piece full of toddy. Then all similar bamboo pieces in which toddy will have been brought are emptied and the contents consumed. The offering known as "Koll" is not so interesting; beaten rice, plantains and jaggery are placed on a plantain leaf at the shrine and the Muppen, after prayers, distributes them.

The Kurichiyans follow Marumakkathayam. They observe Thalikettu Kalliyanam before puberty: all the girls of a Mittam, (group of houses), are brought together, the god Malakari appears in the person of a Kurichiyan and he puts a *thali*—a golden one about Rs. 2 worth—on each girl. Festivities follow, and the next day, the girls go to the nearest shrine and pray, receiving holy water from there. Marriage is permissible before or after puberty, but only after Thalikettu Kalliyanam.

The head of the family is called Pittan and he arranges the marriage. On the day fixed, the party moves to the bride's, with six copper rings, a gold thali for the bride, two white cloths, a coloured cloth and betel and nut. The girl appears, the cloths and rings are then worn by her as also the thali. After meals, the bridegroom's uncle pays Rs. 2 to the bride's uncle for Malakari's favour. The girl is taken to the bridegroom's house and received with lighted lamp and rice placed on a plantain leaf. The bride and seven of her caste-women walk round the light seven times, and they begin praising the girl's beauty, meals are after which served and the guests disperse.

Thirty days' pollution is observed during puberty and the girl has to bathe very early in the morning every day before the men come out of the houses. On the thirtieth day, her female friends rub oil on the girl and give her a bath after which alone can she see a man. The meals on that day are peculiar consisting of "chakkara chore" (jaggery rice), the women first taking their meals and then the men.

The Kurichiyans bury their dead; an arrow is buried with the body if a male, and a scythe if a female. Seven days' pollution is observed and rice is offered to the soul of the departed. The funeral ceremony on a grand scale is observed at any time convenient in the year. They have no priests: the elders act for the occasion. The deceased ancestors are remembered and once a year, toddy, meat, etc., are placed in a room for their use and subsequently enjoyed by the Kurichiyans.

A husband may divorce his wife any time he likes: but the wife has to bring her case before the elders, if she wants to leave him, and they decide the question.

The Kurichiyans are cultivators raising paddy crops on wet lands and raggi on hills. They are also hunters, and in the name of Malakari devote three days—10th, 11th and 12th Thulam (October)—for hunting. They occupy the highest status among the Wynad tribes in point of caste, they do not take meals of any caste but of the Brahmins and the Nayars of Wynad: their houses are polluted if any other caste man should enter the same: and the slightest suspicion is enough to put a man or woman out of the caste. These outcastes have, during recent years, been taken to the Christian fold.

The Kurichiyans are religious, truthful and simple. There were well-to-do men among them before, but they are now in the hands of the clever Moplas who advance them small sums of money until their paddy crops find their way to the Mopla's shop and until in the course of two or three years, they also part with their lands to satisfy their creditors.

It is sad to think of the Kurichiyan's fate. Brought into the country as soldiers, settled here as agriculturists, this race, which a century back had the temerity to defy the British power, has sunk so low that the Kurichiyans find themselves compelled to earn their living as labourers at the beck and call of every one, and unambitious, illiterate and uneducated, they will be dragged lower and lower down, unless something providential happens to help them out of their slough of despond.

Mullakurumbers

Mullakurumbers are bowmen and hunters and, with the Kurichiyans, formed the army of the "Pychy rebel" in his rebellion against the British Power in the beginning of the nineteenth Century. The rebel—Kerala Varma Raja—was killed in 1805 and seven years afterwards the Kurumbers started another

MULLAKURUMBERS.

rebellion which, of course, was instantly suppressed. Their reputation as hunters is still maintained and they fully deserve the compliment given to them by the author of the *Malabar Manual* in the following terms:—" The fact that the Kurumbers preferred a roving life in the jungles to a sedentary one in subjection on the plains, proves them to have been a superior race and indeed to the present day they very markedly retain this characteristic."

According to the chief of this community, their origin was in Puthadi amsam in which the shrine dedicated to their God Kirathan is situated, and they claim to have been—in the spirit world—the *Bhuthams* (Demons), who attended God Siva in his manifestation as Kirathan (hunter) during his hunting expeditions. They are happy in this idea of supernatural origin and have full faith in it, and so mote it be.

The God Kirathan is called by them Puthadi Daivam (Puthadi, lit., *Bhutham-adi*, Demon dance) and while he is their presiding deity, smaller deities known as " Pakam Daivam," "Pullikarinkali," her daughter "Kali," and "Elankuravam" are also worshipped. A place is set apart in their houses for daily worship. The Kurumbers are very religious and in their houses they keep a very small bamboo box called "Pézha" into which every member of the house places from 2 to 8 annas for the deity once a year, generally after the harvest.

They are to be found in Puthadi, Purakadi, Muttil, Kidanganad, Nenmini, Nulpuzha and Kottapadi amsams.

Their chief is styled "Talachil Muppen" and he is the highest authority having jurisdiction over all the *tharas*. A *thara* is a group of about fifty *kuties* (houses) located in a village under the control of a headman known as "Muppen" with a subordinate called "Nalappadi Muppen". Offences against caste and other disputes are reported by the subordinate Muppen to the headman of the *thara* who in the presence of an assembly composed of one member from every house and in the presence of the deity—who is represented by an inspired Kurumben—tries the case and in case of conviction, imposes a fine varying from one to sixteen fanams (fanam=4 annas) on the offender, a portion of the fine being set apart for the deity, and the balance spent in buying cocoanuts which are at once enjoyed by those present. The offender has the right of appeal to the Talachil Muppen whose decision is final. Disobedience results in the offender being boycotted by the whole community.

Their language is Malayalam. A good number of them can read and write. Their *kuduma* (hair-tuft) is in front like that of the Malabar people and they follow *Makkathayam* (succession from father to son). Their marriage ceremony—which is an elaborate affair—deserves notice.

Before attaining puberty, no girl is given in marriage. This period is observed for seven days during which the girl is compelled either to sit on a plank or when walking to wear leaves or some such substance on her feet to prevent her touching the ground. After her bath on the seventh day—which is of course a festive occasion—she is confined to a separate room without being allowed to enter the kitchen or the deity's room. This period of segregation lasts until her future husband enters the room and takes her out.

His difficulties are great. He sends his relations to the intended bride's house with betel and nut to ask for her hand: and they are put off more than once before her parents make up their mind. If the proposal is accepted, the parents in the presence of the neighbours declare their consent to the match, and as a sign of betrothal the bridegroom and the bride wear two peacock feathers in their ears; these being removed only on the wedding day. On this day the bridegroom with his party arrives and is received by the bride's uncle with a burning lamp before them and offering betelnut: the bridegroom with the best-man and the women enter the girl's apartment when the former hands over Rs. 5-8-0 as *kanom* (bride-price) to her uncle and the women bring her out. She is given a new pair of cloth and seated on the mat by the side of the bride-groom. Th entertainments commence, drinking and dancing and then the meal, after which the bride goes with the bridegroom. In the evening, those assembled have their dinner at the bridegroom's and the night is spent in carousal. The next day the guests depart after meals and that night the marriage is consummated. Seven days hence, the married couple start on a visit to the wife's with one hundred *dosas* (rice cakes) and are met by her relations half way, who take charge of the refreshments. Seven days' stay and they return, when ninety-seven new *dosas* are sent with them, and ever after (*D. V.*) they live happily.

If it so happens that the parents refuse consent to the match the man has the option to take her away by force and marry her after a fight,—an interesting survival of an interesting past.

A wife wishing to dissolve marriage may do so by paying back Rs. 5–8–0. To this however the husband is not entitled if he divorces the wife. The first confinement takes place at the mother's and subsequent ones at the husband's house. The wife may either stay at the husband's house or leave it on his death and if she prefers to leave, she is given rice and cloth and the sons are given bows and arrows. A second marriage is permissible but not respectable.

The Kurumbers observe *Vishu* (Malabar new year's day) in April, *Ucharal* in Makaram (February), *Onam* in Chingam (September) and *Sankaranthy* (September). On the first two occasions, they hunt wild-boar for three days and on the last two, they catch birds by bird-lime.

They have paddy cultivation on wet lands and raise hill crops on the slopes of hills. They eke out a small income by husking paddy which they obtain from neighbouring land-owners and the womenkind convert the paddy into rice. They do not generally go out as labourers. Sundays, Tuesdays and Fridays are generally spent in hunting and no work is done then.

They have a gift of prophecy, only some being initiated in the art known as "Kotiveykal" literally, "planting betel vine" The professor when consulted about any future event husks a small quantity of rice by hand, places it inside a scooped-

URALI OR VETTU KURUMBERS.

shell of a dried kuvvalam fruit (*Aegle Marmelos*) and asks one of his men to "plant the betel vine". The man understands the meaning, takes out the rice and spreads it on a plank. The professor invokes the Puthadi deity, makes a calculation and gives his reply which is generally found correct.

The Kurumbers cremate their dead; a bow and arrow, a knife and a betel pouch being kept with a man's body and a scythe with a woman's. Pollution is observed for two days when the nearest relation performs the funeral ceremony and offers a ball of rice to the soul of the departed. Mulla Kurumbers are truthful by nature and uninterfering in their habits. Soldiers in the past, hunters and cultivators in the present day, they enjoy the good things of the world in the limited sphere in which they have been placed under the all-pervading influence of Kiratha Murthi.

Urali Kurumbers

These are also known as "Bet or Vettu Kurumbers" (*vettu*, to cut) from their profession of felling trees.

They are found almost all over Wynad and while they speak Malayalam and Canarese, both in a corrupt form, they speak among themselves a peculiar dialect not understandable by any stranger.

These men are artisans and are handy at all kinds of work. They make ploughs and knives as any black-smith does, earthen pots that last longer than those made by professional potters, cut and size timber just as any carpenter, make umbrellas of screwpine leaves, are skilled in basket work and gather honey from the tallest tree. As agricultural labourers, they are useful and their services are always welcome in tea estates. Many good qualities they have, but they are not a thriving class and are improvident.

Their houses are called *padis* which are so low that one has to crawl into them but the inside is kept clean. They have a partiality for raggi and millet but as a variety eat rice also. They can also subsist on edible roots for any length of time, and such roots being plentiful in Wynad, they do not starve.

The bridegroom's parents have to ask for the bride; all being well, the marriage is celebrated, the expenses amounting only to Rs. 3 to 5. But if the bride's parents object to the match, the bridegroom goes out with his friends and takes her away by force. The bride's parents have then no alternative but to consent after levying a fine from the bridegroom which of course is paid but spent on drink. During confinement, the woman is kept in a separate hut for seven days if the child is a boy and for five days if it is a girl. They follow *Makkathayam* and are illiterate.

The Urali Kurumbers never touch the carcass of dead cattle—in fact do not even touch anything made of leather. If they touch even a shoe they commit an offence against caste for which the elders invoke their God—Masti—to absolve the offender and the occasion is taken advantage of for drinking.

They bury their dead and observe no death pollution; but when funds permit, a pollution feast is held. Uralis are a class of artisans without whom the Wynad people could not, in the days gone by, exist but in the present day they suffer from competition on the part of artisans coming up from the plains. They have therefore, to maintain themselves as labourers whereby they lose their aptitude for work as artisans.

KUNDUVATIYANS

This community consisting of about forty families is to be found only in Puthadi and Purakadi amsams. It is a question whether they are above or below Mulla Kurumbers in social status: they claim a higher position: like them the Kunduvatiyans are bowmen and *shikaris* but are not as adept as they. They have their *kuduma* (hair-tuft) in front and they follow *Marumakkathayam.*

Their deities are Puthadi Daivam, Elavilli and Puvilli, to whom offerings are made thrice a year in the shape of cocoanuts, plantains and jaggery. One from the community acts the priest and on the day preceding the offering, he fasts.

Marriage is permissible before and after puberty. The bridegroom's relations arrange the day of wedding in consultation with

KUNDUVATIYANS.

the bride's. On the day appointed the bridegroom arrives with his party, and hands over to the senior female member of the bride's family a gold jewel worth not less than Rs. 5, bangles and rings and also two pieces of cloth for the bride which she wears, and then sits with the bridegroom on a mat. Festivities commence and the next day all those assembled, proceed to the bridegroom's where they are entertained by his people. The marriage is consummated the same night if the girl has attained puberty, if not, the girl is left with the husband for a few minutes in a room and taken away, the marriage being consummated only after she attains puberty.

Seven days' pollution is observed after puberty and if the purification could not be done then, pollution continues till the twenty-first day. A woman of Perumannathi caste brings a piece of cloth for her to wear and on wearing it (of course after bath) the girl's pollution ceases.

The first confinement takes place at the father's house and there is no particular ceremony observed during the period of pregnancy. The child is named and its ears bored on the thirty-first day.

Divorce is easily effected, and the wife who is divorced may take another husband, but this is not considered respectable. Polygamy is not permitted.

Kunduvatiyans cremate their dead except in the cases of children of three years or below. Both sons and nephews observe nine days' pollution and the eldest of the nephews perform the funeral rites and offer *pinnam* to the soul of the departed.

On Vishu day (Malabar new year's day) meals are placed on nine or eleven leaves and left inside a room, intended for the deceased ancestors: a nazhika (24 minutes) afterwards, the doors are opened and the meals taken out and used by the members of the family.

Kunduvatiyans are cultivators and do not generally serve as coolies. They have their own paddy cultivation from the proceeds of which they maintain themselves.

Caste disputes are decided by four Muppens who have power to fine the offender to a maximum of 120 fanams (fanam=4 As).

KARIMPALANS.

The punishment can be awarded only by all the four Muppens together. Leaving a portion of the fine to their deity, the balance is divided among the Muppens, a system which is sure to increase the number of convictions. The origin of Kunduvatiyans, it has not been possible to trace, but from the fact that they observe *Marumakkathayam*, that they wear *kuduma* in front, that they observe *Thalikettu Kalliyanam* before puberty and that their language is Malayalam, there is every reason to believe that they migrated from Malabar. As likely as not, they were Nayars and their appearance is not against this supposition.

KARIMPALANS

A small community of seven families and thirty-seven souls exist in Kalpetta, Muttil and Purakadi amsams. They are cultivators and hunters like the Kurichiyans.

They have no idea of what their origin was or where they came from. They say that about thirty years ago they were about 150 strong.

They dress like Kurichiyans, have the

kuduma (hair-tuft) in front, follow *Marumakkathayam* and speak Malayalam. They worship a deity known as "Pamburi Karuvan," to whom offerings in the shape of plantains, cocoanuts and jaggery are made once a year after harvest. On special occasions, the ceremony of "Thera" is also performed to propitiate the deity, when the caste-men join in a grand feast. They have no separate priest, no barber, no washerman, but manage all these among themselves. But these Karimpalans' services are utilised to propitiate the deity "Asurakalan," by Nayar families in their neighbourhood and offerings of cocoanuts and plantains are then made to the deity. They also act as *velichapads* [oracles] in the shrines dedicated to Karuvan and Bhagavathi.

They observe the *Sambandham* form of marriage as among Malayalis; the man goes to the woman's house with cloths and betel, presents cloth to the woman, her mother and sisters and takes the wife away the next day to his house. The *Sambandham* is permissible only after puberty. In the seventh month of pregnancy the *pulikuti* ceremony, on the twenty-eighth day after confinement, the ear-boring ceremony on the sixth month, the *chorunu* (rice giving), all these are observed just as in Malabar. They are illiterate.

When the Nayars of Vengapally, Chumbrat and Mambilichi houses start on a hunting expedition, Karimpalans have the right to precede them. Kurichiyans do not generally attend upon these Nayars.

Offences against caste customs are heard and disposed of at a meeting of the senior members of their community and the offender is excommunicated, a feast following the disposal of the case, to give publicity to the excommunication. A woman misbehaving herself with a superior caste does not violate caste customs.

They bury their dead except where the eldest member of a house dies and he or she is cremated.

Hill tribes are gradually dwindling in number, they show no tendency to increase, and Karimpalans with their limited number of 37 have very little chance of continuing long as a community. More is the pity.

KADERS

This community is to be found in Tonder Desam, Terriote and Mangalasseri of Wynad Taluk. They were Nayars who accompanied the Kottayam Raja along with the Kurichiyars and assumed the name of *Kaders* (forest men), as they settled in forests. They worship Mālakari, a manifestation of Siva as hunter.

Curiously enough their house is known as "Illam"—which in Malabar is the name of a Nambudiri's house.

They were the lords of the forest in ancient times, but now while a few of them cultivate wet lands, the majority of them live on hill cultivation and some even work as coolies. They are bow-men and are experts like Kurichiyars in archery.

Besides their god Malakari, they worship another deity Kariyathan.

They follow *Marumakkathayam* and observe some of the customs of Nayars. Paniyars and Naykans have to stand at a distance and they (Kaders) bathe if they touch a Tiyyen—but the Nayars have to bathe on touching them. Between the Brahmins and the

KADERS.

Kaden, there is pollution only at a distance of seven feet.

They do not have the *Thalikettu Kalliyanam* of Nayars. The elders of the family arrange the wedding and the bridegroom and his friends go to the bride's, where they are treated to a good meal: the bridegroom hands over two new cloths to the bride's mother and the girl is then taken home by him. She lives with the husband, and even after his death, she continues to live in his house for one year, after which she returns to her house when she is given cloth and the deceased husband's knife and other belongings.

For puberty there is a five days' pollution and a ceremony at the end in which women alone take part. After confinement there is ten days' pollution but the woman is not allowed to cook meals until the fortieth day.

The rice-giving ceremony is in the sixth month as also the christening.

Kaders bury their dead and nine days' pollution is observed. They are purified on the ninth day when a *Munnuttan* (another caste) sprinkles oil on them. This individual becomes the oracle for the day and represents the deceased. He states his wishes before the festivities commence.

Annually a puja is performed in memory of the deceased, rice-cakes, meat and liquor being offered to the spirits of the deceased and consumed by the living.

Caste disputes are heard and disposed of at a meeting of seven *Karanavers* (elders) of the following families:

Mavaliyen—two members.

Paloten—one member.

Kallanthara—one.

Pilacheriyanmar—three.

The *Karanavan*—senior member—of a family is known as *Piriyen.*

Kaders are generally illiterate, but a few of them can read and write Malayalam.

Pathiyans

A small community of agriculturists of this name exists in the easternmost village (Nulpuzha) of Wynad, bordering on Mysore. Formerly natives of Punnat in Mysore, following the *Makkathayam* law of succession (*i.e.*, in the father's line), wearing moustaches,

PATHIYANS.

and with back-tuft (*kuduma*), but now permanent settlers in Wynad following the *Marumakkathayam* law of succession (*i.e.*, in the mother's line), with the moustaches removed, and with the tuft in front, the history of their evolution is interesting. From Punnat, their ancestors migrated during a famine into Wynad, and being prevented by the Kottayam Raja—the then ruler—from returning to their own country and being ordered to adopt the customs and manners of the Malayali inhabitants, they settled down as agriculturists with the result that their descendants now present an interesting admixture of Malayali customs with those of Mysore. In the law of succession, in dress, in *kuduma*, in the observance of pollution on births and deaths, and in *Thalikettu Kalliyanam*, they follow the *Marumakkathayam* communities of Malabar and they have adopted Malayalam as their mother-tongue, having given up their ancestral language—Canarese—long long ago.

The *Thalikettu Kalliyanam* as observed in Malabar is combined with the actual marriage as celebrated by their ancestors. On this occasion the bridegroom and the bride revert to the customs of their forefathers, and a Mysore Brahmin (*Vasti Patter*) officiates and hands the garlands with which they garland each other. Sixteen *fanams* (Rs. 4) is the *kanam* (bride's price) paid by the bridegroom and at the wedding feast the friends contribute their mite towards a fund which becomes the property of the bride. This marriage does not, however, confer on the children the right of succession; but the wife lives with the husband during his lifetime.

At the wedding while assuming his ancestral costume of turban, cloth and coat, the bridegroom, though unable to restore the lost moustaches, puts the *kuduma* loose on the head so as to make it appear as a backtuft, and the bride, who as a settler in the country had changed her costume, resumes the ancient habit and wears glass bangles on both hands, replacing the silver bangle of Malabar which had till then adorned one of her wrists.

Thus we have a small community of not over 100 families who combine the ancestral

URIDAVANS.

but not forgotten customs of Punnat with those of their adopted country Wynad—a community whose history and traditions are interesting and who as agriculturists live a contented life in this wilderness far removed from civilisation. The Pathiyans were probably Gowdas (Jains) originally, and this belief is strengthened by the fact that a *Vasti Patter* —Jain Brahmin—still officiates at their marriages and that their ancestral costume which they then adopt is similar to that worn by the Gowdas of Punnat. Their name is traced to the order of the Kottayam Raja in Malayalam "*Pathikalayi Irippin*" "(You) shall settle here"; the word *pathi* has different meanings but here it means "to settle" as in the expression "*Kutipathi*" (householder).

Seven days' pollution is observed after death. They cremate their dead and recognise and pray to a deity known as *Melethalachil*, a manifestation of Siva, under whose protection they live as peaceable and law-abiding citizens.

Uridavans

The correct name is evidently "*Urudavans*" —owners of villages. How this community obtained this dignified name is not ascertainable. They claim to be of *Vedar* caste, the same as that to which Arippen and Vedan, the Vedar rulers, belonged. They have nothing warlike about them and their profession—cultivation—is that of peace-loving citizens. They say however that they were hunters before, and it was only after the forests were declared "Reserved" by Government that they adopted the present profession.

Their ancestors migrated from Chittaldroog in Mysore and their first settlement was in Tirunelli. At present this community is to be found in Tirunelli, and in the neighbouring Puthadi amsam.

They are Vaishnavites, have back hair-tuft (*kuduma*) and moustaches, speak Canarese, and follow *Makkathayam*. Their deities are *Karinkali* and *Pakam Daivam* (God of Pakam).

They are agriculturists and reside in houses called *Ure* (village). Their houses are not in groups but scattered, half a dozen or more being in the same neighbourhood. These have a headman—*Ejman*—for each desam (hamlet) who decides caste disputes among the community. The fine varies from two to sixteen *fanams* according to the position of the party concerned and the gravity of the offence. Cocoanuts are purchased at once and broken and offered to Karinkali and Pakam Daivam, the kernel being consumed by the people present.

Three days' pollution is observed during puberty, and marriage is permissible before and after puberty.

An elder member of the bridegroom's family goes with a friend to the intended bride's with betel and nut and asks for the consent of the party. The bride's father consults the relations and the *Ejman* (headman), settles the question and fixes the wedding day.

On the day appointed the wedding is celebrated in the presence of the *Ejman* and the caste men, the bridegroom brings ear ornaments, bangles, rings and cloth, and the ceremony lasts for five days. Their *gurikal* (priest) who comes from Punnat in Mysore and who is known also as "Udayar" garlands both the bridegroom and the bride on the sixth day. The ceremony is over and on the seventh day the priest is paid six fanams. The bridegroom's father pays sixty-five fanams to the bride's father and she is then taken to the bridegroom's house, and on the day of arrival there is a feast.

The third day after confinement the women in the neighbourhood are treated to a sumptuous meal, and the child is named by its father.

The Uridavans bury their dead, but when old men die they are cremated. Pollution is observed for fifteen days and on the sixteenth day, the ashes are thrown into the river—and the ceremony is observed on that day, or on the thirtieth or within the next three months. The priest—*gurikal*—gives holy water and receives his four annas.

They follow *Makkathayam* and the wife lives in the husband's house; after his death she is at liberty to go to her own house and if she elects to do so, she is given a cloth and one rupee. She can marry again, but it is not respectable or proper. It is concubinage. The caste customs do not allow divorce.

THACHANAD MUPPENS.

The community of Uridavans does not exceed more than a hundred families. It is said that seven men with their wives ran away from their native place, Chittaldroog, when there was a battle in that country, and the present generation represents the descendants of those seven families. There is a tradition that they were called "*Odakar*" by the Saktan Raja of Kottayam, as they ran away from the fight (*Odakar*, they who ran). Whatever their real name may be whether Uridavan or Odakar or Vedar, they do not, so far as could be ascertained, belong to the caste to which the proud Vedar rulers belonged.

Thachanad Muppans

Muppainad, the country of Muppans, probably took its name from the Thachanad Muppans who settled in that amsam. Their advent into the country is interesting. Two deities, male and female, known as *Karivilli* and *Manhalapothi* finding no devotees took human forms and induced three Muppans and their wives to leave their native place Nilambur in Ernad Taluk, and proceeding by Matiyaram mountain they came into Wynad. On the way one Muppan and his wife died, so that there were only two couples left. They originally settled down in Muppainad in the localities known as Karangandam and Valathur and the existing community represents the descendants of those two Muppans, they being no doubt supplemented by further immigration from Nilambur.

They are known as Thachanad Muppans and the derivation is probably from Thacharakavil Nad, country of Nilambur Tirumulpad, whose family name is Thacharakavil. These Muppans in smaller numbers still exist in Nilambur where they are known as *kuden*.

Every *padi*, *i.e.*, group of huts, has two chiefs, one for two-thirds of the population of the *padis*, and the other for the remaining one-third; the senior being known as *Muthali* and the junior as *Eleri*. They should be present at every social function and should lead the deputation of Muppans on the occasion of the visits to their Jenmis. They govern the *padi*, punish offences within their jurisdiction, and there is none to dispute. The appointment is hereditary and the succession to the office is from father to son and failing the son, to the brother.

The gods of the Muppans are Karivilli and Manhalapothi, who brought them from Nilambur to Wynad; and the Muppan and his wife who died on the Matiyaram hill on their way have been deified and are worshipped as family deities under the names of *Kurikka* and *Pramanichi*. In every *padi*, the Muthali worships the male deity in his room and the Eleri the female deity in his room, and even now Muppans passing the Matiyaram hill place a stick there as a token of respect to them.

The most interesting part in their lives—as in the lives of all civilised nations—is the marriage ceremony. All the members of a *padi* are considered to belong to the same clan and they cannot intermarry. One *padi* has to find a bride in another and the duty of selection falls on the Muthali and Eleri who proceed to the bride's house on the day fixed. The bride's party (*Pennillakar*) welcome them and the bride stands on a plank facing east with half a rupee on her foot and one rupee on her head placed there by the Muthali of the bridegroom's party (*Anillakar*). These are taken by the bride's uncle and by the party who provide the wedding feast and then the usual payment of Rs. 10 *kanam* (bride's price), Rs. 10 for the wedding feast, and 4 fanams (one rupee) for the bride's Jenmi is made by the bridegroom's party. After prayiñg to the family deity, she leaves with the bridegroom and his party to his *padi* where she is left in the Muthali's room in the presence of his deity *Kurika*. The bridegroom joins her there and the next morning they—husband and wife—after taking their meals in that room with two male and two female friends go to the hut prepared for them.

The young Muppan leaves the paternal roof on marriage and at once builds a hut for himself and his mate—an excellent system which civilised nations may well imitate. A group of such huts forms a *padi* and the number of huts in a group would indicate the number of married men there. The husband with the assistance of three friends could construct the hut in a day or two with split bamboo roof, with bamboo wall and with a thatch of long grass that serves to protect them from sun and rain. There are 18 padis, each padi consisting of 30 to 40 souls, so that in Muppainad and in the neighbouring Kottapadi amsam the Muppans number a little over seven hundred. The *padis* are not fixtures, but are moved from place to place, following the Muppans to the neighbourhood of the land prepared for cultivation.

When a girl attains puberty, the male members do not attend the ceremony. On the seventh day, the women of the neighbouring huts take her to the bank of the river and throw an iron-tipped arrow over her head. She then bathes and returns in procession to the husband's hut, where the women are treated to a sumptuous meal, which, of course, the husband has to provide.

During the wife's pregnancy, the husband grows his beard which is removed only after confinement. This shaving is also a ceremonial act. A lighted lamp is placed in front, as also one *nazhi* (measure) of rice, one cocoanut, betel and nut. The husband pays one rupee, a piece of cloth, 10 seers of paddy and one meal to the woman who attended on his wife during confinement. The wife is under pollution for ten days after which the rooms are purified with cowdung and she bathes.

The rice-giving and the ear-boring ceremonies are generally performed once a year during their annual festival known as "*Pati Attu*" when all the children are brought before the gods. This occasion is also taken advantage of by the father to name the child.

On the death of the wife, the husband performs the funeral ceremonies and is bound to maintain the children, but if both parents die, the father's relations take care of the children and in their absence, the mother's relations. On the death of the husband, the wife at once leaves for her house and after some time returns to the husband's *padi*. On her leaving after the husband's death, his relations give her one pothi (50 seers) of paddy, an earthen pot, a scythe, a spade, a cloth and a bottle of oil.

KANALADIS.

These people do not follow any definite law of succession, but it is understood that they are governed by *Marumakkathayam.*

They speak Malayalam and are illiterate. They live on slopes of hills cultivating small extents of jungle cleared annually. They also work in paddy fields and in tea estates but are generally idle and deceitful, whiling away their time in loafing about, living on edible roots which are abundant in the country. They are dwindling in numbers, are a poor and miserable race with no chance of rising, and with the area of hill cultivation narrowing year by year by the clearing of jungles for tea and other cultivation, their means of livelihood are becoming more and more scanty. The Government have however assigned 326 acres of land for hill cultivation, on a low rate of assessment; but their idle and drinking habits are not likely to lift them up from what they are—a jungle tribe.

KANALADIS

Kanalattam—(*kanal*—burning coal, *attam*—dance) is a religious function among the Hindus. In the plains it is performed by a caste named Malayans and in the Wynad by Kanaladis. Six families—four in Nulpuzha and two in Puthadi amsam—represent the total population of this class in Wynad and they earn their living by acting as "oracles," "fire-walkers" and "devil dancers" during *Thera* festivals at shrines.

They are few in number; the men have to indent upon Mulla Kurumbers, Pathiyan and Chetty castes for wives, and when these classes wish to get rid of a woman, she is welcomed by the Kanaladi, who ties a *thali* round her neck, presents her with cloths and silver bangles and makes her his wife.

They observe eleven days' pollution after death and holy water from a Brahmin's hands purifies them. Cremation is the rule.

Their language is Malayalam: and they have no idea of the law of succession. To hazard a guess, Kanaladis are the descendants of Malayans from the plains, who settled in Wynad long long ago—and took the name of Kanaladis from their inspired feats on burning coals. In spite of this inspiration, the extinction of the community is only a question of time.

ADIYANS.

ADIYANS

The ancestors of this tribe migrated from Coorg. But the only indication of this fact is in the name of their deity *Kuttath Karinkāli*—the first word being supposed to be a corrupt form of a word "Kotaku" Coorg. The headman of Adiyans says his tribesmen are still to be found in that province. They are field-labourers and have also hill-cultivation.

They worship three deities—Karinkali above mentioned, Malakari and Kuliyen. After harvest is the favourable season for the annual offering which is known as *Thera*. At night on the day fixed, one seer of rice, one cocoanut, two plantains and a little beaten rice are placed before a lighted lamp by the *karmi* (priest), and the oracle known as Kanaladi appears with a white cloth on his head and a sash of white and red. He issues his commands and the whole night is spent in drum beating and playing on the reed flute. The next day the *Thera* festival closes.

Marriage is permissible only after puberty. The father and the uncle of the bridegroom go to the intended bride's and fix a day. On that day the bridegroom takes a coloured cloth, a necklace of beads, bangles, rings and Rs. 5-8-0. The first four are given to the bride's mother, Rs. 5-8-0 to the bride's uncle, annas 8 is intended for the bride's Jenmi, and the balance is equally divided between the father and the uncle. The bride wears the cloth and the jewels and sits with the bridegroom on a mat and an Adiyan woman throws some rice on the heads of the happy pair. The bridegroom dines and sleeps at the bride's house and the next morning she goes with him.

During puberty four days are observed as pollution and on the fifth day, the neighbours are all invited to a sumptuous meal.

The Adiyans bury their dead—only very old people "*Muravanmar*" being cremated. If they can afford to indulge in a feast, the funeral ceremony is celebrated on the fifth day or it may be postponed till the fifteenth day after death. The *valiya pula*—grand-pollution—is observed once a year in memory of all the deceased ancestors.

On the mother's death grown up children stay with the father and little ones are taken away by the mother's relations.

Widow marriage is permissible on condition that the bride's price paid originally is repaid to the deceased husband's relations. An Adiyan may have two wives at a time but not more.

As among Paniyars, these Adiyans are given paddy by their Jenmis during Vishu and Ōnam festivals and their women are given new cloths once a year.

The headman of Adiyans is known as Muppan and the next in rank is Mūthali. These titles are conferred by the Jenmi (landlord). Their language is said to be Malayalam but it is a hybrid between Canarese and Malayalam, more akin to Canarese.

They are truthful and trustworthy and do not run away from their employers like the Paniyars. They are to be found only in the amsams of Vemom, Tirunelli, Kuppathode and Puthadi and as agricultural labourers they are very useful.

The law of succession is not very clear. They say that both the sons and nephews share in the property. They have no definite idea themselves but the impression is that they follow Marumakkathayam.

Paniyars

This dark-skinned and curly-haired tribe of a Negroid type is found in all the amsams of Wynad. As agricultural coolies they are a necessity in a country where it is difficult to secure labourers for work in the paddy fields. The tradition about their origin is interesting.

Ippimala, a hill which no one in Wynad could localise and which is said to be somewhere near the Tamaracherry ghats was the home of the Paniyars. They were savage tribes living in caves and thick forests, coming out only at nights and feeding on paddy and other crops. The Gounden landowners finding their crops always destroyed by these black beasts managed to secure a number of them by means of nets known in Wynad as *Thandati* and in six months taught them the language and to go on errands. These domesticated Paniyars induced their friends of the forest to join them, and gradually they spread

PANIYARS.

from place to place until we find them in parts of Coorg and Mysore, and in Wynad and in the hilly tracts of the neighbouring taluks in the plains.

The only reference to the Ippimala tradition now is the word "Ippi" to which the Paniyan gives utterance when he is frightened—say when his master thrashes him.

Their god is Kuli and goddess Kali, to whom and to their deceased ancestors, they make offerings on *Ucharal* day (after harvest) when all the Paniyars of a padi meet to hear the words of the oracle (*komaram*). This is a festive occasion and in addition to light refreshments, arrack is freely consumed, which no doubt increases their religious fervour.

The Paniyars without distinction of sex grow their hair and when too long cut it. The Paniyan shaves off his beard on festive occasions, his wife the Panichi acting the barber and he shaves off the long curls falling on the wife's forehead. Paniyars follow Marumakkathayam.

Marriage is allowable before puberty also.

The bridegroom's father or an elderly relation with a friend goes to the intended bride's and returns without mentioning the subject. He goes a second time and broaches the object of the visit. The marriage is settled and four annas (one fanam) is paid. On the day of the marriage, the bridegroom and his party arrive at the bride's and after they are welcomed, the bridegroom and the bride stand on two bags of paddy. The father or the uncle of the bridegroom pays Rs. 4 as *kanam* (bride's price) to the bride's father or uncle and the bridegroom presents her with bangles and necklaces of beads. They step down and her bag which is smaller, is then tossed to the bridegroom, who tosses it back. This goes on for a few minutes and it is considered inauspicious to let it fall. Of course, the persons standing by, assist.

When a Paniyan decides on marrying, his master gives him 10 *kolakams* (25 seers) of paddy, 5 yards of cloth and 12 annas of which 4 annas is paid on the settlement of the marriage—the balance 8 annas—called "Kappala Panam" being sent through the *Muppan* (headman) of the bride's party to her master.

Paniyars bury their dead and the funeral ceremony falls on the seventh or the twelfth day but if circumstances do not admit of its being celebrated then, it is postponed for six months during which they are under a state of pollution. Their priest is known as "Attali" who sings his prayers during a whole night and then purifies the inmates and the hut. Besides this ceremony a general pollution day is observed once a year called "Kākkapula" (lit., crow pollution) in memory of all the deceased ancestors.

Seven days' pollution is observed after confinement.

There are two *stanams* (titles) Kuttan and Muppan conferred by the Jenmi. They settle disputes and disobedience of their orders results in the offender being fined. In cases of adultery among the Paniyars, a fine of sixteen fanams (Rs. 4) being the bride's price and a sum equal to the wedding expenses is imposed by a council of their headmen.

These Jenmis contribute on festive occasions towards the expenses—and on *Vishu* day—(Malayalam new year) they give a certain quantity of paddy to their Paniyars and in Karkitakam (June—July) present the women with cloths. A Paniyan receiving paddy on Vishu day is not expected to leave his master for the year.

The Paniyars are a necessity to Wynad cultivation; they alone are able to control the wild cattle of this country and in the soft and clayey soil, which sinks to the touch, they alone can handle the plough. Their habits are migratory and unless the employer is kind, they suddenly give him the slip and are not easily caught. In moral turpitude they stand high. They are professional burglars, waylay and rob travellers and do not hesitate to commit the gravest crimes and yet they are excellent-field labourers.

They are fond of music, sing during work in the fields, spend whole nights singing and dancing to the accompaniment of a peculiarly shaped drum and a reed-flute.

With civilisation the Paniyan approaches the towns, drinks his arrack neat, puts a

PULAYANS.

decent covering on his person and understands that the country belongs to the Sircar. The language of the town Paniyan is intelligible though with some difficulty, the jungle-paniyan beats one wholly with a peculiar rush of sounds. It is a corrupt form of Malayalam, mixed however with certain words of unknown origin.

PULAYANS

The Pulayans of Wynad are to be found in the following desams of Wynad:

Vennayote Desam	...	(Kottathara Amsam)
Anoth ,,	...	(Vayitri ,,)
Edachana ,,	...	(Edavaka ,,)
Tharavana ,,	...	(Porunnanur ,,)
Kalluvettumthazha	...	(Anjukunnu ,,)

and they number about two hundred.

It has been found impossible to trace their origin; they say that they were the original inhabitants of Wynad; but their law of succession—Marumakkathayam—indicates a possibility that a colony of Pulayans of Malabar proper migrated into Wynad and settled there. They do not however claim kinship with the Malabar Pulayans and form a distinct sect.

The Pulayans of each desam elect a headman from among them. This headman is known as "Maruthan" and need not necessarily be the oldest member of their community. He is elected by the community for his capacity to govern. His functions are many and varied. He selects the bride for a Pulayan who proposes to enter into wedlock: he obtains the consent of the parents and arranges the preliminaries; pays a sum of not less than Rs. 30 (of course to be found by the bridegroom's parents) to the father, mother and uncle of the bride; and after this payment goes to the bride's house in procession, without the bridegroom. They bring the girl to the bridegroom's house and a week hence, the wife's relatives are entertained in the husband's house and the husband's relatives at the wife's. A peculiarity in the preliminaries to the wedding is that when the Maruthan proceeds to bring the, bride, the bridegroom shall not accompany him, and when he returns with the bride she alone shall accompany him back and not the relations.

Puberty. For seven days the girl is under pollution and on the eighth day a few friends are invited to a feast.

Child birth. For forty days the mother is under pollution and the Maruthan sprinkles *punniāham* on the forty-first day and the pollution ceases. The *punniāham* is composed of oil, turmeric powder, flowers and water. During pollution the mother occupies a separate hut, into which no one may enter except the woman who takes meals to her and this woman also has to be purified on the forty-first day.

Pulayans bury their dead and do not cremate. On the twelfth day the pollution ceases by the Maruthan sprinkling *punniāham* and a feast follows.

Rice giving and naming are done on the forty-first day.

Pulayan's deity is known as "Patha" to whom offerings are made in the shape of cocoanuts, plantains and rice once a year; besides this deity they worship another specially powerful deity "Bhadrakāli" whose very modest shrine is situated in Anjukunnu amsam. The *Velichapad* (oracle) is a Pulayan, who is also designated "Maruthan". This Bhadrakāli is very useful as being able to accomplish any object for which any one makes an offering. This deity is of a malignant character and on proper offerings made causes the death of an enemy from dysentery, and the offerings referred to are arrack, fowls and money of course.

Pulayans are field labourers, a few having their own paddy cultivation. They are carrion-eaters and are considered to be lower than Paniyars who are polluted by their touch. They are generally employed by Moplas as coolies and this is evidently due to their polluting at a great distance the Nayar who could not therefore conveniently employ them in his neighbourhood.

Jain Kurumbers and Kattu Naykans

These two classes of hill tribes are practically identical with some slight differences. The former does not eat monkey's flesh, which the latter does thereby lowering themselves in status. The former gathers honey, the latter does not; the

JAIN OR THEN KURUMBERS.

former does not take meals prepared by the latter, whereas the converse is permissible. Beyond these differences the two tribes are the same in customs, manners and language.

They speak Canarese, and their ancestors migrated from the Mysore forests where this tribe exists in large numbers under the names of Jain Kurubas and Kad Kurubas. Jain is a corrupt form of Jēnu—honey —the same as "Thēn" in Malabar. Their women wear coloured as well as white cloths but more in the style of Mysore than Malabar. They live in *padis* (group of huts) on the slopes of hills under the supervision of Muthali, the eldest man of each *padi*. They worship Masti and live on raggi raised in the jungle clearings and on the edible yams and roots found in plenty on the hills. The Jain Kurumbers would not generally be seen out of the forests, but they are now gradually approaching inhabited parts of the country in search of work in paddy fields. In the Reserve Forests, both these tribes are employed as elephant mahouts.

Caste offences are tried and disposed of at a meeting of three or four Muthalis and the fine which varies from four annas to five seers of paddy is appropriated by the judges. Marriage ceremony is not so elaborate as among certain other tribes.

The bridegroom's father or uncle goes to the intended bride's with a garland of beads, which, if the girl's father consents to the match, is handed over to him. On the wedding day the *Anillakar* (bridegroom's party) proceed to the *Pennillakar's* (bride's party) house with cloth, brass bangles, six brass rings, brass ear ornaments and 8 annas. Both parties together start a dance—*kolkali*—round the girl. The cloth and the jewels above named are given to her and she wears them. The whole party then pray to god Masti, and the bridegroom and the bride ask for the blessing of the Muthalis also. The bridegroom takes the hand of the girl and another dance and the meals follow. The ceremony closes at the Pennillakar's house. The party returns with the bride to Anillakar's, then a dance, betel-nut and meals and the marriage closes

KATTU NAYKANS.

there also. Makkathayam is their law of succession.

A girl attaining puberty is confined to a room for seven days and no man sees her. Green turmeric is rubbed on her person and she is privately taken out by women to the river and after bath is admitted into the hut. Marriage is not permissible before puberty. During pregnancy, her relations give a brass bangle to her and there is no other ceremony. After confinement, the woman is kept apart for three weeks. The eldest son is always called after the grandfather and the eldest daughter after the grandmother.

These tribes cremate their dead except in case of children, who are buried. Two weeks' pollution is observed generally, but none for children. Four balls of rice are offered to the soul of the deceased and also water in a bamboo cup.

Their deity Masti has no shrine. He always lodges in an earthen pot and is represented by arrow root tubers, kept in it. There is a Masti pot in every *padi* and the (*pena*) spirit of the deceased is always sent to keep company with him in the shape of arrow root tubers. The old adage "gone to the pot" has proved true in the case of these tribes.

When they wish to see Masti, all that they have to do, is to open the pot, invoke Masti and sing—when one of the members of the *padi* gets the inspiration—and his commands are respected. Masti has the power to impose fine for misdemeanour of any description among the tribe and every year each *padi* makes offerings to him during the harvest season (*Ucharal*).

These people always carry a stick (*kuzhikole*) in their hands which is intended for digging roots. They strike fire by the friction of two bamboos. A dried bamboo has a hole made in it, a small bamboo piece is inserted and turned and turned until the friction causes fire.

Jain Kurumbers and Kattu Naykans are a primitive race without a history and they are happy in their mountain slopes with means of subsistence always available in the shape of edible roots. Another decade, they will also be working for wages in the tea estates and earning their livelihood like their brother aborigines of Wynad.

TIRUNELLI SHRINE.

CHAPTER VII

THE SHRINES OF WYNAD

1. Tirunelli
2. Vallurkavu
3. Ganapathivattam
4. Manmathan
5. Trimurthi
6. Kalliyanath Palli

TIRUNELLI SHRINE

The *Sthalapurana* of this famous shrine contains the following passage:

Grāmam Sadēvadēvēsam
Tat Kṣhētram dhanasantatim
Rakṣhā sikṣhādhikāram cha
Dēva srēṣthākhya ya saha
Dvigotrēbhyo dvijāgrēbhyo
Dhārā pūrvam pradātavān.

The village was granted with God Vishnu (Dēvadēvēsan), his shrine, its revenues, and power to protect and punish, to the eminent Brahmins of two different families and this grant was made by pouring water into their hands as signifying transfer of proprietorship.

The village referred to is Āmalaka gramam, and the temple, the Āmalaka kshetram or Tirunelli temple, as it is known in Malabar, and the grant was made by Brahmadéva under the following circumstances to the Brahmins who were first appointed as its priests and proprietors.

On the summit of the Brahmagiri mountain, Brahmadéva performed *yagam* (sacrifice), and there Vishnu with four hands bedecked with numerous fine jewels, seated on an Āmalaka tree appeared before him. The figure however suddenly vanished. Brahmadéva then founded a temple at the spot dedicating the same to Vishnu and gave it the name of Āmalaka kshetram or Tirunelli temple (*Tiru*—sacred, *Nelli*—gooseberry tree). Brahmins were appointed priests to whom the temple was entrusted as also the small village that sprung about it, relics of which still exist in the shape of old foundations of houses.

Brahmadéva departed but visits the temple every night to worship Vishnu. The *puja* (worship) in every shrine closes ordinarily at about 9 to 10 P.M. and in this shrine, where the ordinary puja is done five times, from morning till 10 P.M. the priest prepares for a sixth puja before leaving the place. On opening the doors next morning he finds that all the materials for the puja have been utilised during the night. It was Brahmadéva who performed the sixth puja and this has been going on every day and will go on for ever. The priest before entering the temple in the morning swears thrice that he will not divulge what he sees there on opening the door, and no priest dare give out the secret at the risk of being bitten by cobras emanating from the shrine.

Whatever the present generation may think of a superhuman agency performing an unusual sixth puja in this shrine, the fact remains that it is arranged for every night in the belief that Brahmadéva visits the temple and worships Vishnu.

As already mentioned Brahmadéva appointed

Brahmins as priests: but nothing is known as to how they or the gramam disappeared. There is a long blank in the history of the temple and a Sannyasi, who in this wilderness took up his residence in the deserted temple had an inspiration in obedience to which he brought down four Embrandiri Brahmins from Gokarnam (Canara) to take charge of the temple.

The puja was naturally neglected during the Mysore invasion but subsequently the *Sannyasi*—known as Samiyar—returned. He found one of the Embrandiris returning with another person, who was the ancestor of the present Uralers (trustees). To them the Sannyasi handed over the temple, the Embrandiri to perform the puja and the other individual to manage the affairs. Subsequently the manager claimed proprietorship and succeeded in establishing his right. His family was divided into north and south branches, represented by Vatakku Moothannan, and Thekku Moothannan, the present (*Uralers*) trustees of the temple. The junior members in their families are known as Elayannan and Kunjannan. They claim kinship with the Musads of Malabar and follow their customs and manners as in Malabar proper, the name Moothannan being composed of *Moothathu* (*i.e.*, Musad) and *Annan*, evidently a courtesy title common in Coorg which province adjoins Tirunelli amsam.

The idol is of granite stone and is said to be of excellent workmanship. After destruction by fire during Tippu's invasion the temple was first reconstructed with thatched roofs. The *Srikovil* (central shrine) has since been roofed with copper and surmounted by a golden spire. The ground in and out of the temple is paved with granite stones.

Shrines and sacred springs surround the temple and a brief description of the same is extracted below from the *Malabar Gazetteer*.

"At the back of the temple a stream of clear water comes tumbling down from the hill-side in a succession of pools and cataracts, and many of these pools are holy. Their names are *Papanasini*, the extinguisher of sins, *Panchatirtam*, *Rinamochinitirtam*, *Gunnikatirtam*, *Satavinnu*, *Sahasravinnu* and *Varaham*. The water of the last is brought for temple use in a stone aqueduct half a mile long. The water of Papanasini falls on a rock called Pinnapara where offerings to the spirits of the departed are made. This rock is a bone of an *Asuran* or demon, named Pashana-bhedi, slain by Vishnu, whose body was at his own prayer converted into a rock extending from Tirunelli to Gaya, Tirunelli representing his foot, Godaveri his middle, Gaya the head. Just by Gunnikatirtam is a small cave temple dedicated to Siva."

Besides the above, there is the *Pakshipashanam* (lit., bird-rock) called "*garudappara*" (Garudan's rock) beneath which are found several interesting caves known as Pathalam (nether world) where hermits in the ancient days lived and which as the story goes, were visited by Mr. Baber, Sub-Collector of Northern Division, Malabar, in the beginning of the nineteenth century. He met the hermits and built a flight of steps for them to climb up to their caves, the cement used being still visible in parts. The Bavali river deserves mention as derived from *Vari*—water and *Avali*—collection—collection of waters—the right name of the river being Varavali. The junction of Nanda stream with the Bavali is known as Nandabavali Sangamam and is a sacred spot where low castes who are not allowed to enter the temple make their offerings. On the eastern side of Gunnika temple is a rock on which Sudras perform funeral rites on the forty-first day after the death of their relatives.

The *Punarjanini* (re-birth) has a sacred function attached to it. This is a cave in the rock with opening on two sides, and any person who is stuck midway in attempting to pass through is considered a sinner, and his way of escape out of the difficulty is by praying to God Vishnu when he could retreat. It is only one free from sins, and sincerely devout, who need attempt to pass through scatheless.

The above is a brief notice of the famous Tirunelli shrine—"the resort of many a pious Hindu under the promise of remission of sins and eternal bliss". Its sanctity, antiquity and divine origin have never been disputed by Hindus—and it is a matter of regret that the two copper plates preserved in the temple and the inscription on the granite wall could never be deciphered as those would have given a clearer idea as to the origin and history of this famous shrine. As it is, one has to depend on the "Stalapuranam" (local legends) for information and this is given here as succinctly as possible.

THE VALLURKAVU SHRINE

The following brief account of the above shrine appears in the *Malabar Gazetteer*:—

"About two miles from Manantoddy on the banks of the river is the Vallurkavu, the famous fish pagoda, dedicated to Durga and supposed to have been one of the four shrines erected to protect the Tirunelli temple. The Carnatic carp and other fish in the pool of the river adjoining the temple are sacred, and to feed them is a method of acquiring merit. This fact points to a Dravidian origin of the temple. Possibly it was at one time a temple of the Valluvars, a servile caste of labourers and fishermen. Thousands of pilgrims come for the temple festival which is held in March."

Local tradition points to a quite different origin which, as will be seen from the following account, is traced to Kotungallur (Cranganore) in the Cochin State.

Nalveettil Nambiars (lit., Nambiars of four houses) are the Velichapads (oracles) attached to the Cranganore temple. They lead an itinerant life and live on the offerings they receive from the Hindu houses. In their perigrinations they carry with them a sword, which as an emblem of the deity, serves as an easy passport for their livelihood. In the olden days, two such men arrived in Wynad, with the object of visiting the holy shrine at Tirunelli. One morning they left Manantoddy for the temple, but having missed their way found themselves in a thick jungle. The heat of the sun was intense and the stream in the vicinity tempted them to take a plunge therein. They performed the usual puja to the sword, took light refreshments and leaving the sword in the adjoining ant-hill, rested in the

VALLURKAVU SHRINE.

delightful shade of the thick foliage of trees and were soon in the arms of Morpheus. When they awoke they found the sword missing and a search was made with no effect. Meanwhile a Kurichiya boy who was grazing his cattle brought the happy tidings that a sword was seen suspended on a creeper on the adjoining hill. The pilgrims hastened to the spot and tried to take hold of the sword. It would not leave the creeper in spite of their efforts and they noticed the sword rising higher and higher in the air the moment they attempted to touch it. In appealing terms they addressed the sword and repeated several times the words "Valliyur Amma"[1] (O Mother! disentangle thyself from the creeper). These entreaties were not responded to and the pilgrims left the place in sad disappointment. The matter was reported to the local chieftains, Edachana Nair and Vemoth Nambiar, on whose visit to the place, the sword was found in the same position. They attempted to touch the sword and it dropped

[1] Valliyur—*Valli*—Creeper, *Ure*—to draw or to let go.

down, sticking fast in the ground. The miraculous incident was reported to the Raja of Kottayam, then the ruler of Wynad. The Raja's visit to the spot was followed by oracular utterances from a *Velichapad* (oracle) in the following terms:—"I desire to settle in the locality in three different places and in three different forms: first as "Vana Durga" in the place where the sword fell, as "Jala Durga" in the pool of the adjoining stream and lastly as "Bhadrakali" in the middle of the above two places and a temple should be erected with the four eaves of the roof projecting into the four oceans." The Raja expressed his utter inability to undertake the construction of a temple in the manner indicated; whereupon the goddess declared that no edifice was then necessary and she would prefer to remain exposed to the sun and rain. After this incident, the Raja made arrangements for the daily puja, which was entrusted to Cherangote Nambidi, Edachana Nair and Vemoth Nambiar who were appointed Managers. The three centres specified in the divine message are to this day held sacred and none ventures to pollute their sanctity either by hunting in the adjoining jungle, being the abode of Vana Durga (*i.e.*, Durga of the forest) or fishing in the stream below, wherein the Jala Durga (Durga of the water) is supposed to reside. The ant-hill on which the sword rested prior to its disappearance, is known as Maniputtu (*Puttu*—ant-hill) where puja is performed during the days of the annual festival. Just in front of the Maniputtu is the Kali's shrine which remains closed, except during the fourteen days of the festival. It is here that during the last three days of the festival the Cherangote Nambidi (priest) exhibits to the public the exact form of the goddess, as appeared to him in a vision, hence the name "Oppana" by which the exhibition ceremony is termed. It is interesting to note that people from all parts of the Taluk, nay from the plains also, throng to the temple with the most anxious expectation to have a look at the "Oppana," the prevailing idea being, that one blessed with the sight of the deity in this form will be free from all epidemic diseases during the year.

GANAPATHIVATTAM TEMPLE.

The above legend throws much light as to the true origin of the shrine. Vallurkavu (lit., Valliyurkavu) took its name from the passionate appeal to the deity by the pilgrims in their endeavour to regain the sword.

The English name of the shrine apparently originated from the fact that fishes in the pool which is considered sacred are left there without molestation, for fear of incurring divine displeasure.

There is a general impression that Vallurkavu is one of the protecting shrines of Tirunelli Temple. This cannot be right, as the former was but of comparatively recent origin after the Kottayam conquest. As regards the reference to Valluvars, however interesting it may be philologically, there is nothing in Wynad to show that they ever existed in Wynad. The origin of the shrine, as traced to Cranganore, is accepted as correct by the faithful votaries of Durga.

Ganapathi Vattam Temple

This is a melancholy chapter to a Hindu who has faith in Ganapathi, son of Siva. When he sees that his image is mutilated and his temple ruined, he feels that divine beings with divine powers have, like human beings, their own seasons of adversity which they cannot avoid.

An arrow from a huntsman's bow was the immediate cause of Sri Krishna's death—or rather disappearance from the world—and all must bow to fate, and the Ganapathi at whose shrine every inhabitant within a radius of about 12 miles prays, suffered the indignity of the mutilation of his idol which, as a visible and tangible symbol to the ignorant, had been placed in the temple to represent him. Ganapathi Vaṭtam—the sphere of the Ganapathi, covered the amsams of Kidanganad, Nulpuzha and Nenmeni and when Tippu of Mysore overran the country, his troops destroyed the temple and mutilated the granite idol. The town then took the name of Sultan's Battery and the Moslem town of that name sprung up at the time.

In spite of these misfortunes, Ganapathi's influence has not waned. The Wynadan Chetti, the Mulla Kurumben and the Pathiyan of the three villages named above still believe in him. They have their local gods and goddesses at their own centres but Ganapathi is the overlord who is propitiated by offerings at certain seasons of the year.

Who knows whether Tippu Sultan did not suffer for the sacrilege? That he repented to a certain extent at least is proved by the grant of lands to the Temple free of tax, and this no doubt is a satisfaction. His career of destruction was brought to an end not very long after by the avenging Christian who was considerate in dealing with the Hindu faith and who confirmed and continued the Inam (free of assessment) grant of lands made by Tippu. The tolerant Hindu thanks both for this consideration.

The legendary history of this temple is unknown, but its reputation as one of the famous temples of Wynad deserves at least this small note.

THE GOD MANMATHAN

Manmathan is another name for *Kamadéva* (Cupid) but the Manmathan of Nenmini amsam, presiding over the destinies of Wynadan Chettis, is a different deity and does not pretend to be the God of love.

Manmathan the subject of this sketch is known in Canarese as "Bomma Deva" and has no temple built for him. He is supposed to reside on a small raised platform by the side of the road from Sultan's Battery to the Nilgiri boundary, four miles from the Battery town. He has no image or idol to represent him but is supposed to be there, either on the platform itself or on the *shampak* tree standing on it. The platform is protected by a wooden railing.

Once a year the Chettis perform puja (worship) about June and as the deity is fond of plantains, the inhabitants of the neighbourhood, Chettis, Mulla Kurumbers and also Nayars, offer plantain bunches. The method of selecting such bunches is peculiar. When the date of the festival is fixed, the inhabitants intimate to the Chetti Pujari (priest) that an offering has been made. The Velichapad (oracle) who represents the deity on the occasion then goes round to each garden, picks out the best bunch and removes it. The plantain tree cannot be cut: it can only be pulled down, the use of knife being prohibited.

Numbers of such bunches are thus laid at the shrine for about three days and the influence of Manmathan is so great that no thief would venture to remove them: and no cattle would eat them. The Revenue Inspector—a Graduate—was present at the last festival and affirms that cattle approach but never touch the plantain.

Another peculiarity is that the Deity's mother-tongue is Canarese. Probably he, like so many others, migrated from Mysore. The Velichapad (oracle) who is generally a Chetti converses—when under inspiration—in the Canarese tongue, though he himself does not know the language, a wonderful feat indeed.

The inhabitants respect and esteem him and in every plantain garden in the neighbourhood one tree is set apart as his, so that thieves may not interfere, and this method is found very effective. The bunch is sent to the shrine during the annual festival, so that Manmathan gets a special bunch of plantains for protecting the garden against theft and another as an ordinary offering for the general welfare of the people.

Trimurthi of Manikunnu

This mountain about 500 feet above the level of the Wynad plateau and situated in Kottapadi amsam has the honour of having on its crest a shrine where the *Trimurthis* (Brahma, Vishnu and Siva) are jointly worshipped. It is rather rare to find the creative, the preservative and the destructive powers at one and the same shrine, and according to the legend, it was the great Manu who dedicated the shrine for the joint worship of the three powers. Three idols stand on a rock on the crest of the hill and on *Utharaphalguni Nakshatrom* (star) day of the month Meenum, (March—April) the puja is performed by a Nambudri Brahmin from the Calicut Taluk. On this day the consolidated puja for all the 365 days in the year is performed and the votaries coming in from different parts of the amsam fast until it is over. A peculiarity attached to this shrine is that while there is no water on the top of the hill or anywhere in the neighbourhood, water flows on that day from a cavity in the rock which is dry at other times in the

KALLIYANATHA PALLY.

year. The appearance of water in the hottest part of the year on the top of a hill and through a fissure in the rock is a miracle which cannot be explained except by attributing it to the divine power of the gods that preside there. The correct name of the hill is *Manikunnu* which in course of time has become Manikunnu. It is inaccessible all the year round and the track is cleared on this day for the convenience of the worshippers. The Uralen (trustee) of this shrine was Kottayil Nayar from whom Krishna Goundan, a wealthy land-lord, purchased it with his other properties, and this gentleman now supervises the ceremony and provides a feast on the completion of the puja to the faithful worshippers who attend.

Kalliyanatha Pally

This is a mosque, the proper name of which is Kalliyana Pally, derived from *Kalliyanam*—marriage—and so called in commemoration of the day on which the site of the mosque was granted by the Nayar at whose house there was a kalliyanam ceremony on that day.

Once upon a time, as the story goes, a Sheik was found by the Kurichiyans of the locality seated on a rock near a stream in the Perinchola forest with two tigers, one on either side. The Kurichiyans reported the discovery at Chovvel Edam, the house of Alanchery Moopil Nambiar, who proceeded to the spot with his neighbours. The Sheik was not to be seen but the next day the Nambiar again went in quest of the Sheik, who was then found on a hill. On being asked who he was and what he wanted, he said he had no special object in visiting the place and that he was a traveller. It struck the Nambiar that there was something saintly in this personage and desirous of testing him, he asked the Sheik if he could cure a lady in his house who had been ailing for six years and who was also blind. The Sheik asked for water to be brought and the Nambiar supplied milk. The Sheik repeated certain *mantrams* (incantations) over it and on the same being administered to the lady, she recovered her health and her eye-sight.

The Nambiar asked the Sheik what he

could do for him, when he applied for sufficient ground to build a mosque and he pointed out the junction of the three desams (Edavaka, Ozhakodi and Edachana) as the place he desired. Edachana Nayar, Alanchery Nambiar, Vadikolla Nambiar and Mechilatan Nayar came to the spot and formally made a gift of the site to the Sheik, who then disappeared suddenly.

A few days afterwards, the Sheik reappeared with a few fakirs, who built a mosque, which was an unpretentious affair at first, but in course of time, the Nayars of the locality finding that offerings to the mosque resulted in the accomplishment of their desires granted more lands.

The Sheik and all the fakirs died, the last of them handing over the deeds relating to the mosque-site and the lands to a woman known as Kakka Pathu who was living with her husband in the neighbourhood. They went to Nadapuram and handed the deeds (cadjans) to a Mopla named Ekoten Tharuvayi, who came to Wynad and erected a substantial building. He thus became the proprietor and his descendants are the present trustees of this mosque.

Kalliyana Pally is the oldest mosque in Wynad and the Mopla colony round it consisted of people whose ancestors came from Kadathanad (part of Kurumbranad Taluk).

The date when the mosque was originally built cannot now be ascertained: but as Edachana Nayar and Alancheri Nambiar were chieftains appointed by the Kottayam Raja after he conquered the Vedar rulers, it may be presumed that the Sheik appeared in Wynad during the Kottayam supremacy. Every religion tends towards the same goal and the Hindu and the Mussulman joined in venerating the saintly Sheik—a sign of the spirit of the times when all religions were tolerated.

CHAPTER VIII

LEGENDS AND ANECDOTES

1. Vālmīki's Hermitage.
2. Bānāsur of Mahabharata.
3. The Hermit's Curse.
4. The Pēria Saint.
5. An Ingenious Lady.
6. A Royal Vedar Lady.
7. Ancient Boycott.

Legends transmitted from generation to generation undergo change in course of time, and to prevent these from being entirely forgotten, I have recorded them here, in the hope that they will be entertaining, if not instructive.

I have attempted to connect Mahabharata and Ramayana with Wynad: to identify Pulpalli with Sage Vālmīki's hermitage where Sita lived in exile: and to identify

Bānāsur as the scene of the *Bāna Yuddha* (War with Bāna) of Mahabharata. If they are not true, an explanation ought to be forthcoming why these localities should have been named after Puranic characters and why these legends should have been fabricated. No purpose is served by calling a mountain by the name of Bānāsur, unless the giant himself had built, or was supposed to have built his fort there, and while not prepared to substantiate the truth of the legend, I would ask the readers to leave it as an open question whether the heroes of Mahabharata and Ramayana visited Wynad or not.

Vālmīki's Hermitage

The name Sasi Mala represents a hill in Pulpalli desam of Puthadi amsam in Wynad Taluk. The correct name is *Sisu Mala*, literally, infant's hill. The infants referred to were Kusa and Lava, the twin children of Sita Dēvi, born in Vālmīki's hermitage, during her exile from Ayodhya (Oudh). The hill was called after them, as there they seized the horse sent out by Rama during the *Aswamedha Yagam* (horse sacrifice) and kept their hold till Rama himself came and recognised his two sons. The exact spot is said to bear the marks of a horse's hoof and the hill has since borne the name of "Sisu Mala".

At some distance from it is the hermitage —a cave, where Vālmīki is supposed to have been seated in *tapas* (meditation) and this is now blocked up by ant-hill. The rock just above the cave was the spot where Lakshmana alighted from the chariot with Sita. A shed stands on the rock, the thatching of which is to be completed in a day, *i.e.*, from morning till evening. The tradition is that as the work is finished wild dogs would chase deer into the shed, kill it and leave it as a remuneration for thatching the shed. The dogs have not been so accommodating for some time past.

The twins, Kusa and Lava, are worshipped under the name of Munikanmar—*Muni-Kumaran-mar* (children of the Sage) and Sita under the name of Chedattil Amma. The temple is situated about four miles away from the rock above mentioned.

The water of the stream near by is said

to have been yellow as Sita used to bathe in it after confinement. This colour was attributed to the turmeric used by Hindu ladies on these occasions but lapse of time evidently restored the water to its original colour. There is however a peculiar sort of paddy known as *vari nel* grown in the neighbouring jungles. No seed is sown: but a very small quantity is found in patches supposed to have been the remnant of the paddy used at the hermitage.

The temple with its properties is known as Pulpalli Devaswam and the Uralen (trustee) is Kuppathode Nayar. He claims descent from the *demoiselle de honneur* who accompanied Sita from Ayodhya in her exile.

A short note on Sage Vālmīki by Rev. Munro Taylor is appended for the information of the reader.

"An ancient Sage: an ascetic who continued so fixed in one place and posture, in his penance, that *termites* threw up their diggings around him; so that he appeared to be seated in an ant-hill, whence his name. At what time he left it is not stated, but he had a hermitage; and one day walking from it to gather fire-wood, heard a bird on a tree utter sounds, which he reduced to writing and found they formed a *sloka*; in which measure he, or some one in his name, wrote the Ramayanam: the Sanskrit poem being often mentioned with his name prefixed, to distinguish it from the Telugu and Tamil versions. In his advanced age when Sita was repudiated by Rama, she dwelt in the hermitage of Vālmīki, and therein her two sons Kusa and Lava were born."

Bānāsur of Mahabharata

The height of Banasur mountain is 6,762 feet and the *Malabar Gazetteer* mentions that "a legendary giant is said to have built a fort on it".

This giant is known as Bānāsuran, a giant who by austere penance (*tapas*) acquired such powers that Siva had to be warder of his palace. His lovely daughter Usha fell in love with Aniruddha, grandson of Sri Krishna. Their clandestine meetings came to the notice of Bānāsuran, who clapped the lover in prison. Krishna having received intimation of this incident proceeded to rescue him and was met by the giant and by Siva, who was compelled to assist the former. Naturally, it was an open question who would win, and at last when no weapons were found to be effective Siva sent "Siva Jwaram" to annihilate Krishna's army. This was met by Krishna's "Vishnu Jwaram" which rendered Siva's weapon ineffective and threatened to destroy the whole of Bānāsuran's army. A compromise was effected and Usha left for Dwāraka as the wife of Aniruddha.

Thus runs the tradition as described at length in the Mahabharata and the fort of Bānāsuran is said to have been on the Bānāsur mountain.

The giant's arms were chopped off by Krishna during the fight, and a temple called Karabanasseri exists at the foot of the mountain where daily puja (worship) is still being performed. An annual ceremony is performed when a member of the Munnutten caste in the dress of a hunter known as Malakari plays an important part. Karabanasseri temple is supposed to commemorate the cutting of the giant's arms (*Kara*—arm, *Bana*—Bānāsura) and the Malakari represents Siva as the guardian of the *Mala* (mountain). Closely connected traditionally with Bānāsur is Mazhuvannur—about 8 miles away—in Porunannur amsam, where there is a Siva temple indicating the place where Siva's battle-axe fell, in the course of the fight. *Mazhu-vanna-ure* (lit., axe-came-village) was called after the axe that was dashed out of Siva's hands at Banasur.

Inferences are not always correct: but some may be amusing owing to their absurdity. The compiler of Mahabharata could not have been aware of the malarial nature of the Wynad climate. But Siva Jwaram is known also as *Ushna Jwaram* (heat-fever) and Vishnu Jwaram as *Sita Jwaram* (cold-fever): the two expressions representing the fever prevailing in the plains, and the ague existing in Wynad. Krishna's Vishnu Jwaram having prevailed against Siva's Jwaram, ague, attended with chill, prevailed in Wynad. Malaria is thus traced to a divine origin but, medical opinion may not agree with this conclusion.

The Hermit's Curse

At Sultan's Battery in the Wynad Taluk nearly two furlongs to the south of the town and a few yards south of the sixtieth mile stone on the Mysore road, stands a *vasti* temple, a magnificent and an interesting relic of the Jain colony that lived and flourished here years ago, and then became practically extinct. The neighbourhood is still known as "Annaradu Vithi" which in Canarese means 12 streets indicating the colony of Jains that settled there, and the tank which they used for bathing purposes was called "Dodappan kulam" which however can hardly be identified, as it has been gradually filled up with earth brought in by the heavy monsoon. The place is deserted but the inhabitants of Sultan's Battery would point out where the street and the kulam existed. The families that settled there became extinct and the few who survived left the place so that there are no Jains here now. The cause of extinction of a flourishing colony is believed to be the following: A Sannyasi (hermit) finding his way to the village, handed over a pot to one of the

RUINS OF JAIN TEMPLE.

residents and asked him to keep it till his return. The man hung up the pot in his room and after a few days found that the pot was slightly leaky, and the droppings, which fell on the iron utensils and agricultural implements, converted them into gold. The pot was found to contain liquified gold and it was at once freely utilised by the members of the Jain community to convert all the iron they possessed into gold. The house in which the pot was kept was then set fire to and the gold buried in the ground. The Sannyasi returned and on asking for his *kanakam* (gold) pot, was informed that it was lost in the fire. He then cursed them: "The treasure that you have buried knee-deep in the earth shall not be found and this city shall become a ruin." Thus was the colony of the Jains ruined and the large quantity of gold which even now is believed to exist underground never discovered. In fact several attempts appear to have been made to get at the hidden treasure but none was successful and the Moplas of Sultan's Battery have been anxious to secure the temple site, which however has been reserved against such alienation.

THE PĒRIA SAINT

The Pēria saint was a Pathan who with his brother came into Malabar from the north. The direction "north" is vague, but it is supposed to be near Delhi. One of them died at the Pēria ghat and was buried at the spot where the tomb exists on the slope of the hill. He has been canonised and Mussalmans hold him in respect. Some one had the ingenuity to build an auxiliary tomb on the road side in a line with the real tomb, so that votaries may conveniently make their offerings there instead of having to climb up the hill.

He must have been fond of cattle during his life in this material world and he must also have been a patron of cartmen. At Nedumpoyil valley the cartmen purchase a couple of sandalwood perfumed wicks for lighting at the tomb situated on the road side. This offering is intended to propitiate the saint and protect the cattle, goods and the cartmen themselves from all evil during the journey. The auxiliary tomb can be seen at the twenty-eighth mile stone from Calicut. And he stands as the guardian saint at the gates of the mountain range, ready to protect people from the evil effects of the Wynad climate, of course for a consideration in the shape of offerings.

No one remembers seeing him, but in dreams, he appears in the form of an old Mussalman—grey and full bearded—to those faithful votaries, who make vows to his shrine. So says Ahmedsa, an old Pattani (Pathan) of Manantoddy who has very great admiration for the saint.

It is not only the Mussalman who venerates the saint: in fact it was a Tiyyen contractor who repaired the tomb recently for some benefit obtained through the influence of the saint.

This is the history of the Pēria saint whose tomb on the road side is decorated with small red flags and there we shall leave him—*requiescat in pace.*

An Ingenious Lady

In Chapter III it has been mentioned that the Kurumbala Division of Wynad was placed under Avinjat Nayar by the Raja of

Kottayam. The traditionary account of this delegation is interesting.

The Raja of Kottayam and his consort Lekshmi Kettilamma of Avinjat family on their way to Avinjat house in Kurumbranad Taluk passed through Kurumbala. When they crossed the Malankara river on the west, they noticed that a jackal drove away the dog that accompanied them and began trotting before them. They were on foot and had travelled three *kathams* (12 miles) and when they arrived at the south-eastern boundary of Kurumbala, the dog drove the jackal away.

The Kettilamma was observant and felt these signs as significant and peculiar. They however proceeded on their way and arrived at the Lady's Avinjat house.

That night the family deity of Avinjat appeared before the Lady and advised her to ask her Royal consort for the land where the jackal drove away the dog. The request was made and the Raja complied with it. "You and your progeny shall rule over this country. You shall be I". Thus was made the royal gift.

The Avinjat Lady and her descendants became the Rulers of Kurumbala—the three *kathams* of country where the dog-jackal incident took place.

When the Raja and the Lady returned to. Kottayam, the princes and the princesses protested against the grant. The lady was grieved but as she was sleeping, there was again a dream: in fact an inspiration by the family deity. "Do not be grieved. Promise that you would give up the whole country except Pamben Kuni and Chemben Chira situated west of the Kurumbala fort." She accordingly promised that with these two exceptions she was prepared to give up Kurumbala. There was a conference among the princes and the princesses: they were not aware that Pamben Kuni was a barren and rocky hill and that Chemben Chira was a small tank. They, however, knew the lady to be clever: and suspecting that these two places were very valuable, resolved on asking the Raja that they would be content with Pamben Kuni and Chemben Chira. On this being communicated to the

Raja he accepted the proposal and she graciously withdrew her claim to those two spots. The original grant of Kurumbala excepting the two places mentioned above was then confirmed by royal mandate.

"You and your progeny shall rule over the extent of three *kathams* of Kurumbala excepting Pamben Kuni and Chemben Chira. You have all the powers of sovereignty (lit., you shall be we) and shall protect the 299 Nayars, the deities, the Payyerpati Swarupam, the ten houses of Taragans and you have full powers of receiving *Raja-bhogam* (tribute) and shall protect and punish. You shall be *Melkoyma* (the superior authority)."

The Avinjat Nayar thus became Vazhunnaver (ruler) of Kurumbala with the two chieftains Poyil Nayar and Thenamangalath Nayar under him.

The Kurumbala Nad now consists of Kurumbala and Kottathara amsams and the southern portion is under the Kuthali Nayar to whom it was given by Avinjat.

This tradition is interesting as showing how a clever lady secured the sovereignty of a country from her husband, outwitting the junior members of the royal family by asking for a barren hill and a useless tank and then as a matter of grace giving them up when the princes under a misapprehension claimed these for themselves. The hill and the tank still exist—the former measures 76 cents and the latter about 10 cents. No one wants them and the deluded princes and princesses lost a large country through the ingenuity of a lady.

So was the world, so it is, and so will it continue to be.

NOTE—The dog-jackal incident related above would appear to be rather strange but a similar incident as between a hare and a dog is reported in the *Times of India* dated 19th October, 1910, under the heading "The Ruins of Humpi" referring to the capture of Anegundi by Mahomed Tughlak in 1338 A.D. and the appointment of Deva Raja as his Deputy.

One day when out hunting Deva Raja, the Governor of Anegudi, "was astonished at observing that a hare, instead of fleeing from the dogs, attacked and bit them. Marvelling what this strange incident might portend, the king consulted the sage Mādhavā Chārya who dwelt on the bank of the neighbouring river. The holy man said the omen was propitious and advised that a city should be built on the spot". This was done, as also a temple in honour of the sage.

A Royal Vedar Lady

Eravi was the sister of the Vedar Ruler. She was a pious lady. Her jewels were so costly that by the sale of one of her *thodas* (ear ornaments) she was able to found three religious institutions. These still exist and bear her name.

1. Eravimangalam Temple in Anjukunnu amsam.
2. Eravimala in Tavinjal amsam.
3. Eravinallur in Kuppatnode amsam.

She was of Vedar caste and could not enter the temple precincts: but was a devout and sincere worshipper. She was anxious to see the image: but the stone known as Velikal stood in the way. She stood before the Eravimangalam temple at a respectful distance and being unable to see the image owing to the above obstruction, prayed to God for the grant of her wish. She had faith, the stone slanted of itself and the image became visible: she saw: she prayed and her object was accomplished and her faith rewarded.

The remaining *thoda* was presented by her to Eravinallur Temple and is said to be still in the Temple tank. This is the tradition about this worthy lady. In Chapter II "Ancient History" reference has been made to the daughter of the royal Vedar race who was married to Nanthillath Nambiar, the Ruler of Veliyambam. Could the two have been identical?

ANCIENT BOYCOTT

The Raja of Kottayam was coming up the Kuttiyadi ghat with a detachment of Nayars when four of them deserted the main body at the Niravil stream. The Raja dubbed them "Niravil Thetti Nayars" (Nayars who left at Niravil). These deserters however made their way to the top of the Kuttiyadi ghat and settled down there and their descendants representing about fifty houses are still to be found within six miles of Koroth, even their kinsmen in Kurumbranad having severed all association with them. Desertion on the line of march had its own punishment. These Niravil Thetti Nayars are now known as "Niravil Nayars" but they resent being so called.

In this connection it would be amusing to know that this Raja named the chieftains under him by the position they occupied during an engagement.

Pilākīzhu Nayar—Nayar who stood near the Pilavu tree (Jack).

Mulliyankīzhu Nayar—Nayar who stood behind Mulli (Ridge).

Vāzhathattil Nayar—Nayar who stood behind a Vāzha (Plantain tree).

Ālattil Nayar—Nayar who climbed up the Āl tree (Banian).

Ālanchari Nambiar—Nambiar who stood against the Āla (cattle pen) and so on.

CHAPTER IX

HUNTING IN WYNAD

1. Tiger-hunt.
2. Boar-hunt.

A TIGER-HUNT

This is a pastime of a socio-religious character indulged in by Wynadan Chettis, Pathiyans and Mulla Kurumbers. The Chetty takes the lead: but the Pathiyan and Mulla Kurumban have their parts to play. All these inhabit the country round Sultan's Battery, and on information received that a tiger (or panther) is lurking in the jungles, they organise a tiger-hunt and arming themselves with spears proceed to the spot. The surrounding places are cleared, the ground is prepared for fixing stakes and the tiger's refuge is surrounded by a wall of rope-netting six feet high.

Chettis, Pathiyans, Mulla Kurumbers and able-bodied men of other communities guard the net with their spears. They wait until the presiding deity appears in the person of a Chetti; a Pathiyan or a Mulla Kurumban also may act the oracle. The Chetti invokes Manmathan, the Pathiyan invokes Mudiyen Puli—tiger destroyer—and the Mulla Kurumban his Puthadi Daivam (God of Puthadi).

The oracle walks round the net thrice and throws a stick into the jungle and this is followed by stones and sticks from the besiegers, who begin shouting at the top of their voice, calling out to the tiger to come out. He steps out of the jungle, sees the spears pointed at him, clears the space between himself and the net, and makes a desperate attempt to break through the ranks of the enemy receiving thrust after thrust until he dies.

The tiger becomes sacred after death: every one present touches him, women with their children come in and do the same and the long hair on the tiger's face is surreptitiously removed and preserved as charm.

The sport is over and the feast follows. This is provided by the Chettis of the neighbourhood from subscriptions from those who attend and it is generally a success, since the arrack shopkeeper of Sultan's Battery makes an unusually large profit on the occasion.

Boar-Hunt

Boar-hunt on the Thulāpathu day is an institution in Wynad, as it is also in some Taluks in the plains of Malabar. Thulāpathu is the 10th of Thulām, Malayalam year, and falls in October, the exact date in 1910 being 26th. The hunt continues for four days and this account was written on the second day of the boar-hunt.

Besides being a pastime, it has both a religious and political significance; under the feudal system of bygone times the lord of the Manor—to use the English phraseology —starts on a regular hunting expedition, with his armed retainers attending upon him. The system has died out in the present day: but vestiges of it remain, one of which is the boar-hunt on Thulāpathu and the three ensuing days.

In the morning, the huntsmen begin to gather at the house of the chief and on the present occasion it was at the house of Kuppathode Nayar, whose ancestor was one of the leading chiefs under the Kottayam regime and a wealthy Jenmi: by twelve noon, the number of huntsmen, Mulla Kurumber and Kurichiyans number about fifty—and it is said they muster a hundred—and more some times.

All those who attend are fed—the feast being particularly decent—and the huntsmen, with a member of the chieftain's family to represent him, and some Nayar neighbours who naturally join the expedition—start out.

Bows and arrows, and muzzle loading guns are the weapons used—and after a while, the boar being spotted, the Kurumbers start the Tally-ho. A thick bamboo forest but the huntsmen do not care. No boots, no shoes, and with naked feet they chase the boar through the forest. The boar finds its way to the next hill and the huntsmen follow, the boar retraces its steps and the Kurumber's arrow speeds with unerring aim, the boar slackens his speed, the dogs are on him and the Nayar's shot rings out: and the boar falls, to rise no more.

The boar is carried to the top of the hill, where there are a few granite stones, marking the place where the puja (worship) is to be performed. The Kurichiyan or Kurumben starts up inspired and the hunting deity Malakari (Kirātha—Siva as hunter) expresses himself pleased. The Nayaṛ representative of the chief thrusts his knife in and the huntsmen commence operations.

The boar's head is intended for the deity, a small portion of the meat is taken out, salted, dried and preserved in a pot until next year. It is taken out, cooked, and presented as an offering to the deity on the next Thulāpathu day. The hind quarter is set apart for the chief. One fore quarter goes by right to the person who had the first shot and in the present case, to the Kurumber. The rest is apportioned equitably among the huntsmen.

The hunt continues all the four days, the huntsmen being fed by the chief.

Every year on the 10th of Thulām the boar-hunt goes on and this institution is kept up as a pastime and as a relic of the glory of the past.

CONCLUSION

I have executed the work that I set myself to do. I have done my best with the limited materials at my disposal and I trust that, however imperfect it may be, the information contained in this book may, besides being interesting and useful, tend towards the better understanding of a tract of country, which owing to its inaccessibility and its malarial climate, is shunned by the inhabitants of the plains.

INDEX